MY *Life* ON THE *Prairie*

FERN MILLER NILSON

Cover Picture
First frame house built in Stratton.
Served as Post Office, Store, and Home.
Courtesy of Stratton Area Chamber of Commerce.

This Book
is dedicated to
My Son
Edwin Erick Nilson
who helped
make this book possible,
and
to my friend Lucy,
who encouraged me
to write my story.

Copyright © 2013 Fern Miller Nilson
Printed by Copycat Printing
Cover Photograph Credit:
Printed in the United States of America

ALL RIGHTS RESERVED

No part of this publication may be reproduced, stored in a retrieval system or transmitted, in any form or by any means – electronic, mechanical, photocopying, recording, or otherwise – without prior written permission.

ISBN: 978-0-615-83933-2

Contents

Preface vi
The Journey to the Prairie 1
The Homestead 3
The Move to the Farm 4
Education 6
Railway Mail Service 7
My Parents' Farm 8
The Wedding 9
Spring of 1923 10
My Life on the Prairie Begins 12
My Country School Years 14
A School Day in the Country School 18
Eighth Grade Graduation 34
Family Life at Home 36
Telephone 38
Early Automobiles 39
Early Lighting 41
Saturdays 46
Early Christmases 52
Michigan 53
New Transportation 56
Invention of Grain Bin on Combine 57
The Miller Wonder Feed Mill 59
My Father Builds His Shop 60
The Miller Garden Weeder 61
Corn Harvest 62
Wheat Harvest 64

The Depression Years 67
Food From the Farm 68
Autumn 73
Swinging in the Elm Tree 74
Wild Flowers 76
Family Trips 77
Mother 81
Blizzards 83
Dust Storms 86
The Miller Basin Tiller 90
The Miller Rod Weeder 91
Floods 92
Our First Tornado 95
My Father is Protected 95
Another Storm 96
Lightning 97
Other Disasters 98
The Weather 99
Other Business Interests 100
The Miller Disc 101
The Business is Sold to Maurice 102
Stratton High School 103
College Days Begin 104
Teaching 105
The Country School teacher 113
Our Family's Christian Faith 116

Preface

My life on the Prairie began in 1924 and now all these years hence I can see how the hand of God has moved and directed my life in ways I could never have imagined or dreamed. From my early years on a farm where droughts and tornados and floods were real dangers, to peaceful moments in the orchard or swinging on a porch swing, I lived a life of wonder and hope. I could have never imagined that my early years of walking to a one-room country schoolhouse would prepare me to teach students not much younger than me when I was 18 years old.

And then my life, much as depot stops on the Burlington Northern train line, found me moving to new places and experiencing new gifts from God's gracious hand. It is true that we take the bitter with the sweet, yet I see that God indeed tempers the wind on the shorn lambs in springtime.

And so it is my Life on the Prairie has come full circle, back to Nebraska, back to my memories…Yet, I am and always will still look ahead to the life to come when the meadowlarks sing as the wheat turns gold come summer and the Goldenrod blooms this fall…and even when the snows are deep and the stars wheel across my prairie skies.

My Life on the Prairie

The Journey To The Prairie

Southeast of the thriving little community of Stratton, Nebraska lay a farm cut out of the prairie a few years earlier. The little town had been established by early day settlers, mostly from European countries.

Grandpa and Grandma Miller

Coming to the Nebraska prairie was a long journey for my grandparents, John and Louisa Miller. It began in Kisa, Sweden in 1886 by a grandfather who was twenty-four years of age and eager to come to America because he thought there were more advantages here and better opportunities. He had not been married long and did not tell my Grandmother before their marriage of his intentions to leave for America. They came with a nine-month old baby in their arms.

Before leaving, they signed the record book in the church where they had attended. It is still there to this day. They left Sweden for America on April 16, 1886.

It was a rough, three week's trip across the Atlantic. Their fare was cheaper because their vessel was a stock ship in poor condition. The ship was condemned after docking in the New York harbor and was not put out to sea again.

Coming into port, they exchanged the Swedish Kronor they had left for $28.00 in American dollars. The adjustment to a new country and language was not easy. At first, all they could do was "point to things" when they went to the store.

On the way to America, my grandfather became acquainted with three other men who were going to Edgar, Nebraska to work on the railroad section. Grandpa decided to join them and paid one man $4.00 for his job. This was their first introduction to the prairie lands of Nebraska.

Grandpa worked about four or five years for the Burlington Railroad. He also worked in the coal shed filling tenders on the train with coal at the division line at Edgar. Money was scarce so Grandma took in washings using a wash-board for scrubbing. My father, Gustaf Emil Miller, was born at Edgar, Nebraska on March 31, 1890.

The Homestead

While in Edgar, Grandpa Miller became acquainted with a man named Glacier who had a homestead at Stratton, Nebraska. He had homesteaded a quarter section of land (160 acres) with a tree claim by planting five acres with maple, ash, and mulberry trees. My grandfather bought his relinquishment tree claim for $200.00. He also acquired another adjoining tree claim to the south and later added a third quarter and fourth quarter to the farm. The last quarter was mostly pasture for cattle and horses. The other quarters were for farming crops.

The Homestead Act of 1862 stated that a free quarter section of land in the West could be obtained by anyone who would settle on the land beginning January 1, 1863. Homesteaders were required to live on the land for five years during which time improvements must be made. That was our nation's way of getting pioneers to come to the Midwest to plow up the ground and plant crops. The gift of 160 acres of free land was a tremendous force in bringing the homesteaders to the Midwest. The prairie was mostly level land covered with native grasses. Without trees, these early settlers built their homes out of blocks of sod cut out of the land. Sod houses were cool in summer and warm in winter. As the trees grew, they produced wood for building, wood for heating, shade for livestock, and fruit for eating and drying. The best way to save fruit for winter use was to dry it in the sun.

Railroads were also given a large amount of land for

the building of railroads.

They were granted every other section along a rail corridor. It was called "checker-boarding." Land grants encouraged higher quality work, since the railroads could increase the value of the land by building better track. Railroads were a large force in settling and improving the prairie as they brought supplies and mail to the early settlers and also became the means of shipping their crops to the east when they eventually had surplus to sell.

The Move To The Farm

My grandparents moved to the farm near Stratton in the spring of 1892, arriving on March 16th of that year. My father was two years old. At first, the family lived in a dugout in the east end of the pasture on the farm that my father later purchased. A sister was born in the dugout on September 15, 1892. The depression of the dugout in the ground is still visible today.

Many mortgages are recorded in the Hitchcock County Court House where the land was purchased. The many mortgages taken out in acquiring my grandparents' farm indicate the scarcity of money. My grandparents had practically no money to invest in the land and were dependant on money from any crops and livestock they sold to pay off the mortgages. It is surprising that they acquired as much as they did. They worked hard, were frugal, and are to be admired by their descendants. The early settlers all had large families to support.

They raised horses to work on the farm, livestock

to supply their milk and meat, chickens for eggs, and planted large gardens. Later fruit trees in an orchard would supply them with fruit to eat and can. They had to be self-sufficient to supply their needs. A windmill pumped water for the home use and for the animals. Water was also pumped into tanks in a "milk house." The water kept their food as cool as possible. It took a lot of food to feed their large family. Each one had to do what they could to help with the work.

Grandparents' early home built in the 1890's

At first the family lived in a shack on their land, later building the two story home on the same site. There were no buildings on the land, so they had to build a barn for the animals, a granary for storing crops, and other out buildings that were needed. Six more children were born, making a family of nine brothers and sisters. One child died in infancy.

One of my uncles was injured when a farm disc ran over his foot. Someone had to go to town by horse to get a doctor to come the five miles to their home. The foot had to be amputated. The boy was laid on their table as the doctor did the amputation. At that time there were no modern medicines for killing germs or anesthetic to kill pain, yet he survived and later got an artificial foot.

They farmed with horses using walking plows and walking cultivators, usually pulled by two horses. Grandpa bought their first tractor when Dad was 20 years of age.

Education

When he was five years old, my father began attending school in the country schoolhouse located south of their homestead about ¾ mile away. The school was called Pleasant View School, District No. 34. Dad went to school until he was 14 years of age, which was through the 8th grade. One teacher taught all eight grades. There were about 20-25 pupils attending school each year in the little schoolhouse. It was so crowded that the students had to sit on a bench. School was in session five or six months a year. When not in school, my father worked on the farm.

My Father's Country School

Dad had a wonderful mind. With his 8th grade education, he later worked in the mail service on the Burlington passenger trains, became a farmer, and later was an inventor of many farm machines. He manufactured the machines he invented.

As the boys grew older, they needed to find jobs outside the farm. My father's older brother learned about a job in Anderson, Indiana where the Gospel Trumpet was printed. While there he met his wife who had come from Michigan to work in the same company.

Railway Mail Service

My father loved the railroads. At the age of 20, he decided to go into the Railway Mail Service, taking the mail service exam on November 10, 1910. It was the next spring before he received his grades from the examination. There were 210 who took the exam. Only four came out ahead of my Father; moreover he stood 4th at the top of the register. Grandpa had said my father would never make the grade. When my father came out fourth, Grandpa was quite impressed. The grade that pleased Dad most was the perfect score of 100 in Geography. It was most important to know the locations of towns and states when working mail. At that time, mail was to reach its destination as soon as possible, sometimes being delivered on the railroad line.

After receiving a telegram from the Chief Clerk of the Railway Mail Service to report for work, Dad took a trial run, round-trip, from Omaha to Denver. He worked several runs before being given a regular appointment to the Omaha-Denver main line, which he worked several years.

As a mail clerk, he sorted the mail in the mail car and put it into sacks. Outgoing mail was put in a mail bag at each town. This mail bag was then put on a crane beside the track to be picked up by the train as it passed through the town. A mail crane (or arm) on the mail car reached out and grabbed the bag. Mail bags to be delivered to the town were thrown from the mail car onto the ground. On a few occasions the bag would roll back under the wheels of the train and the bag of mail would be cut to pieces.

Dad remained in the Railway Mail Service from 1911-1916. The mail service always had a special place in his heart and he never lost his love for trains. In 1916, Dad quit the mail service because he had a chance to buy a farm.

My Parents' Farm

Across the road from Grandpa Miller's homestead was a farm homesteaded by O.R. Jones. He had homesteaded the land free for growing a tree claim on it for five years. Dad and his brother, Oscar, bought this farm together in 1916. They paid $12,000 for five quarters of land. The two brothers lived on the farm and farmed it together until Oscar went into the military in 1918. At that time, Dad bought his brother's share of the farm and later added on to it in 1937.

The Wedding

My mother and father's wedding picture

When Dad's brother, Carl, went to Indiana, he had met my mother's sister, who also worked at the Gospel Trumpet. They were married and had moved back to Nebraska to live on a farm south of where the grandparents lived. My mother came to Nebraska from Michigan to visit her sister. While in Nebraska she met my father. They were married on Thanksgiving Day in 1918 in my grandparents' home. So, the two sisters met and married the two brothers. Mother made her wedding gown. After the wedding my mother and father left by train for Michigan where they spent two months with Mother's family, returning to Stratton in early 1919 to live on the farm that Dad had previously purchased. An old house stood in the center of the land near an ash tree. The ash tree lived as long as my parents did. It was about the only tree that we children climbed up into.

My mother found the old house needing much cleaning when she arrived from their honeymoon. She was determined to make it spotless and neat, but she despaired of the bed bugs that had taken up residence in the house before she came to Nebraska. She told of her struggle to get rid of them. She would take a feather dipped in kerosene (coal oil) each morning and clean the bedsprings until the bugs were all gone. My older sister, Edna Lois, was born in this house on January 25, 1922.

Spring Of 1923

Fern (left) and Edna

In the spring of 1923, my parents began construction on a new house just to the south of the old house. They moved into the new home in the fall of that same year. I was born in the new house in 1924. Always, as I grew up, I thought it was the finest home in the area. I greatly admired my mother and father, their abilities and their position in the community. As a business man, my father was always well thought of. Everyone recognized my parents' high moral standards. I never heard anything unpleasant said about them.

Mother had lived in Ohio and Michigan before she was married. She was not used to the vast open plains. How she missed the trees she grew up with. Perhaps that is why she spent so much time and energy planting trees, flowers, and putting in a nice lawn.

Maurice (left) and Verna

My sister, Verna May, was born on December 15, 1928 making us a family of five. Then, on April 19, 1932, Edna and I came home from school one afternoon to find we had a baby brother, Maurice Edward. Ours was a good family and we loved each other dearly. My childhood was a happy time; I never questioned but what it was just perfect. We did everything together as a family unit.

The farm I grew up on was southeast of the thriving little town of Stratton, Nebraska. It had been cut out of the prairie a few years earlier. It lay south of the Republican River, up on the divide. It was here I was born on June 29, 1924, to my parents, Gustaf Emil and Hazel Edna Miller. Gustaf's parents had come from Sweden for a new beginning in America; Hazel had come to visit her sister. Life gave her a new beginning in Nebraska, a beginning that lasted for 50 years as my parents lived in the same house they built in 1924 and farmed the land. Those 50 years have such a wonderful story to tell. This is where I, too, had my beginning of experiencing a full, rewarding life that has covered almost 90 years as I now write the story of "My Life on the Prairie."

My Life On The Prairie Begins

On a Sunday in June, Dr. L. L. Brown came out from his office in Stratton to deliver my little life. I was born on June 29, at 8:00 a.m. and weighed 7 ¼ pounds. Fern Finch, a friend of my parents who lived on a farm about 11 miles away, came to be my nurse. She helped to take care of the family while my mother was in bed recovering. I was given her name, "Fern", so I became her namesake. Written in the cover of my baby book she wrote:

> *"To my dear little namesake*
> *Fern Loree Miller.*
> *May the blessings of God be*
> *upon you, and may your life*
> *be one of service for the Master."*

Fern Finch was also the Cradle Roll Superintendent at the church we attended in Trenton, Nebraska.
She sent this when I was one year old:

> First Birthday Greeting
> *Member of*
> *The Cradle Roll*
> *Every bird that sings above,*
> *Tells you of a Father's love,*
> *Blossom sweet, and sunshine mild*
> *Cheer and bless you, little child!*

> Second Birthday Greeting:
> *Member of*
> *The Cradle Roll*
> *Suffer them to come*
> *In their childhood undefiled*
> *see the loving Master welcomes*
> *To His arms, each birthday child*

My middle name, "Loree," was chosen because it was the name of my mother's friend in Ohio. So, it came about that I, who was born that warm day in June, was named "Fern Loree Miller."

My mother recited a lot of poetry to us. When I was small, she often quoted this:

> *"Monday's child is fair of face,*
> *Tuesday's child is full of grace,*
> *Wednesday's child is full of woe,*
> *Thursday' child has far to go,*
> *Friday's child is loving and giving,*
> *Saturday's child works hard for its living,*
> *And a child that's born on the Sabbath day*
> *Is fair and wise and good and gay."*

As a young child, I went with my family to the Church of God in Trenton, Nebraska. The church was 11 miles from our home. Sunday School was special for me because my earliest Sunday School teacher was Fern Finch, who I was named after. She had our little Sunday School room set up with a precious worship center. As I recall, there was a little

Our Farm House

altar and backdrop draped with white satin. I thought it was beautiful.

From my early childhood and throughout all the years that followed, we always wore our best clothes to church. We were taught that God deserves our best, our respect, and our devotion.

Wildflowers grew along the roadside. One Sunday as we drove home from church, my father stopped along the road to let us children pick the wild blue spider plant that was blooming so profusely along the roadside. Little did I know that a sticky substance would ooze out of the stems and get all over my pretty Sunday coat. I was a very sensitive child and felt so badly because I thought I had ruined my coat.

My Country School Years

I was only five years old when I began walking

the mile to our country school to attend first grade. I attended the same school district, Pleasant View School, as my father did when he was a boy. The school grounds covered about five acres and were taken out of

Fern in Country School (Front row, second from right)

the southeast corner of my parents' farm. It was called "Pleasant View School" because our farm was called "Pleasant View Farm." The buildings consisted of the schoolhouse, a coal shed for coal and corn cobs for building fires to heat the schoolhouse, and a lean-to barn where horses could be stabled if students rode horses to school. Only the John Wyss' family sometimes rode horses as they were quite a distance from school.

For many years, my Mother, Hazel Miller, was on the School Board in our Pleasant View District serving as treasurer. Though the district only held school for eight months a year, and though the teacher's salary usually was $60-$65 per month, many teachers would come to our house to apply to teach in our country school. The teachers had to pay their own room and board and would often stay with school families.

School started the first Monday of September and usually ended about April 20th.

Classes ran each day from 9:00 in the morning until 4:00 in the afternoon. Because all eight grades were taught by one teacher, classes usually ran about 5-10 minutes in length. During all my eight grades at country school, there were four of us in my class—Evan and Warren League (twins), Howard Wyss, and me. The families in the school included those of Andrew Hawkinsons, John Wyss's, Bill Wyss's, Ray Leagues, Floyd Leagues, Jesse Hudsons, Ivan Ruggles, the Masseys, and our family, the Gustaf Millers.

There were two outhouses on the farthest corners of the grounds, one for girls, one for boys. It was very cold walking to them in the winter. The toilet paper we used was pages from Montgomery Ward and Sears Roebuck Catalogs.

Our schoolhouse was heated by a coal-burning stove at the back of the room. Not only did the teacher have to teach all eight grades, she had to clean the schoolhouse each evening. It was also her responsibility to get there each morning early enough to get the fire started in the stove so the building would be warm when we children arrived. We knew the teacher was at school when, from our house, we could see smoke coming from the chimney. To start the fire, she dipped corncobs into a can of coal oil (kerosene) and placed them under the coal. The corn cobs burned easily and started the coal burning. During the cold of winter, our ink often froze in the ink bottles or inkwells on our desks during the night. It thawed as the room warmed up. Those who sat at the back of the room near the stove kept the warmest. If it was too cold, sometimes we all had to gather around the stove to keep warm. Children in some country schools took potatoes to school for lunch. They baked (cooked) them on the heating stove and had a warm lunch. We children sometimes carried a thermos of hot cocoa in the top of our lunch bucket for a warm drink at noon.

We carried our noon lunch in a lunch pail or a sack, and our water to drink in a Karo syrup pail. There was no water on the school grounds. We had to carry all we would use during the day for drinking and washing. Lunches consisted mostly of sandwiches, cookies, and fruit. Often we took jelly sandwiches, sometimes it was peanut butter. I did not like jelly sandwiches because the jelly soaked into the bread. It was a treat to have roast beef slices with dill pickles or roast beef and pickles ground up between our bread. Occasionally, when a ring of bologna was only 29 cents, Mother would buy a bologna ring that we sliced and put between bread slices. A piece of chicken with a dill pickle was also very good and a treat. If we did not have anything to put in our sandwiches during the Depression days, we ate onion sandwiches, and I thought they were good. Much of the year we did not have fresh fruit so we took a small jar of canned fruit. When bananas sometimes sold for 5 cents a pound, we had a banana in our lunch pail.

My first grade teacher was Velma McCue. Other teachers included Zilah Bailey, Mrs. Willard, and Miss Cesler. I liked school and was a good student.

On the first day of school we left home with a Big

Chief tablet on which to write our lessons. We used pencils to write with and usually also had an eraser, and a box of crayons. When we were older, we also needed a bottle of ink and a straight pen with pen points, and perhaps a box of paints for artwork. When we got to school, each of us chose a desk that would fit our size. Desks were of all sizes, the older students got the long, large desks. The younger ones fit into the small desks.

The recitation bench was at the front of the schoolroom. It was long enough to hold all the students in a class. Most classes were not very large. There were four in my class all through grade school from grade one through eighth grade.

When it was time for our class, the teacher called us up to the recitation bench. We usually had 5-10 minutes for a class. There was very little time for discussion. Usually the time was spent handing in our work and being given the new assignment.

Our subjects included Reading, Arithmetic, English, History, Geography, Spelling, and Penmanship. But we also had classes in other subjects like Mental Arithmetic, Civics, Nebraska History, and Art. The reason we must learn all the subjects well was because before we could graduate from the eighth grade, we had to take county exams in all the subjects and pass them.

A School Day In The Country School

Opening Exercises

When the school day started, it began with Opening

Exercises. The teacher either read from an interesting book or we sang songs. The teacher had a small phonograph that played the accompaniment to many of the songs we sang. We used a yellow book of "Favorite Songs." We also sang patriotic songs like "My Country 'tis of Thee," which was our national anthem when I was in country school.

MY COUNTRY 'TIS OF THEE

"My country, 'tis of thee, Sweet land of liberty. Of thee I sing;
Land where my fathers died, Land of the pilgrims' pride,
From every mountainside, Let freedom ring!
My native country, thee, Land of the noble free, Thy name I love,
I love thy rocks and rills, Thy woods and templed hills;
My heart with rapture thrills, Like that above.
Our fathers' God, to Thee, Author of liberty, To Thee we sing;
Long may our land be bright With freedom's holy light;
Protect us by Thy might, Great God, our King!"

Other patriotic songs we sang were "America, the Beautiful," "Battle Hymn of the Republic," and "The Star Spangled Banner."

We sang many southern songs like: "Yankee Doodle," "Old Folks at Home," "Dixie," and "My Old Kentucky Home." We also sang rounds of music with "Three Blind Mice" and "Scotland's Burning."

On Fridays, we had Current Events for opening exercises. Most of the time, we just gave a headline or told about a short news article.

We also began the day saying "The Pledge of Allegiance." At that time, the words "under God" were not included in "The Pledge of Allegiance." The addition of the phrase, "Under God," to the Pledge was done by Congressional Act, and was signed into law on Flag Day, 1954, by President Dwight Eisenhower. These words had their source in Abraham Lincoln's immortal Gettysburg Address:

"…we here highly resolve that these dead shall not have died in vain—that this nation, UNDER GOD, shall have a new birth of freedom and that government of the people, by the people, for the people, shall not perish from the earth."

Grades were given by numerical numbers like 99, 93, and 100 instead of letter grades.

Reading

After opening exercises, our first class of the day was Reading. The beginning grades learned new words by flash cards. Their first stories were about Dick and Jane. "See Dick. See Jane. See Dick run. Run Dick run." The story continued as they learned new words.

There were Reading books for each grade as the children grew older. Stories went from "The Story of the Three Pigs," "The Three Bears," "Little Red Riding Hood," "The Little Red Hen," and on to "Cinderella," "The Gingerbread Boy," and "The Billy Goats Gruff."

By the time we reached the sixth, seventh, and eighth grades, we were reading "Jack and the Beanstalk," "Aladdin and the Wonderful Lamp." "Hansel and Gretel," "Rumpelstiltskin," and "Snow White and the Seven Dwarfs," Our class time was mostly devoted to reading a portion of our assignment out loud to see if we could pronounce the words and were reading well. We did not spend much time on reading comprehension.

Our small country school did not have extra books to read like Black Beauty, Treasure Island, and Robinson Crusoe. Some of us never did go back and read those books because we soon were reading high school literature.

History and Civics

The next class for the older grades was History or Civics. We learned about Columbus leaving Spain in 1492 with three ships—the Santa Maria, the Pinta, and the Nina. We learned that they thought the world was flat because they could not see beyond the horizon. They were looking for a shorter route to India than going around Africa. When they finally sighted land after leaving Spain, they called the people "Indians" because they assumed they had come to India.

Later, we studied about the Pilgrims coming to the new world on the Mayflower in 1620. They landed north of where they had planned to land. They settled at Plymouth Rock during a cold, dreadful winter and found Indians their only neighbors. These Indians turned out to be a blessing as they taught the Pilgrims to plant crops and to hunt the wild animals. As a special project, we wrote a story about the Pilgrims and put it into a booklet.

Next came the Revolutionary War when the colonists wanted their independence from Britain. They chose George Washington to be their Commander-in-Chief to lead the Revolutionary army. We studied Paul Revere's midnight ride to warn Lexington and Concord that the British were coming. Just as Washington became our President during a critical time of setting up our government, so Lincoln also became President when slavery was a pressing issue between the north and the south.

Above the blackboard were portraits of George Washington and Abraham Lincoln to remind the students of their important part in the founding of our nation. Between them was the flag of our nation. We also studied about Thomas Jefferson, Benjamin Franklin, and other important leaders and their role in establishing this new nation.

In Civics we learned about the Constitution and the Declaration of Independence.

We were taught how Presidents were elected and how Congress made our laws.

Nebraska History

We also studied the history of Nebraska. We needed to learn about our prairie settlers, how they withstood prairie fires, blizzards, sickness, loneliness, and a multitude of hardships like plagues of locusts and drought. All of this added to the hazards of early farming in Nebraska.

Settlers came west in covered wagons with what few provisions they could bring with them like bedding, utensils, basic food supplies, and a plow. They had left their homes in the east to build sod houses on the prairie. They brought the plow to turn over the soil so they could plant crops. Many of these early settlers stopped in the new state of Nebraska where the land was fertile. They utilized the Homestead Act and began building farmsteads as they plowed up the ground. The western part of Nebraska saw increased settlement when the serious Indian wars ended about 1880. These prairie settlers persevered and made the prairie state of Nebraska an important part of our nation.

All of the settlers' work was a back breaking task but they were determined to succeed. Sod houses were replaced by homes built of wood; one-horse plows were replaced by machinery pulled by tractors; transportation saw the Model-T cars replace the horse and buggy; railroads were built making it possible for towns to spring up across the prairie supplying the settlers with needed supplies; schools and churches were built to educate their children and guide their faith. Improvement seemed to abound everywhere. Students learned how our state was established, and how it developed into the dream their parents had as they came west by horse and wagon.

Nebraska was admitted to the Union on March 1, 1867. The name, Nebraska, came from an Indian word meaning "flat water." It is the tribal name for the "Platte River."

The State Bird is the "Western Meadow Lark."
The State Flower is the "Goldenrod."
The State Tree is the "American Elm."
The State Motto is "Equality Before the Law."
The State Nickname is "The Cornhusker State."

Arithmetic

After morning recess, we had our arithmetic classes. The small children learned simple number problems by using flash cards Problems like 1 +1=, 2+1=, 2+3=, 5+2= and so on. As the years progressed and they moved to higher grades, the problems became more difficult.

I loved working arithmetic problems. We worked difficult addition and subtraction problems. Then, we learned multiplication tables from 1 to 12 in every combination. We used these tables to work division and multiplication problems.

Then came fractions, percentages, and story problems.

I was glad when it was too stormy to go outside to play at recess and noon, so I could go to the blackboard to work long division or multiplication problems just for the fun of it. When I was at home, my father often asked me to check out records like bank statements to see if they were correct.

We also learned Roman Numerals. I would write each Roman Numeral up to 1,000 and beyond. The teacher gave us mental arithmetic problems to see if we could follow through and come up with the correct answer. These were more simple equations like 3 x 5, plus 10, minus 3, plus 2. We had no algebra or geometry in country school.

Lunch

At noon, we ate our lunch at our desks and drank water from our pails of water. Then, we went out to play until the teacher rang the bell to come inside for afternoon classes.

English

After lunch, we had our English classes which varied from grade to grade. The upper classes learned the different parts of speech and how to diagram simple sentences to more complicated ones. We learned how to use the tenses: present, past, and past participle and which form of word to use when speaking and writing.

During my years in country school, my teachers had us study some of the famous poets and their writings. I so much liked many of the poems and came to appreciate not only the poems they penned, but the subjects they wrote about. In school we learned some of the great poems from memory. They became a part of my life and have stayed with me all down through the years. I can still quote many of these poems.

I especially liked **"The Children's Hour"** by Henry Wadsworth Longfellow as he told about the eventide when the father comes home to be with his children.

THE CHILDREN'S HOUR

"Between the dark and the daylight,
    When the night is beginning to lower,
Comes a pause in the day's occupation,
    That is known as the Children's Hour.

I hear in the chamber above me
    The patter of little feet,
The sound of a door that is opened,
    And voices soft and sweet.

From my study I see in the lamplight,
    Descending the broad hall stair,
Grave Alice and laughing Allegra,
    And Edith with golden hair.

A whisper, and then a silence:
    Yet I know by their merry eyes
They are plotting and planning together,
    To take me by surprise. . . . .

I have you fast in my fortress,
    And will not let you depart,
But put you down into the dungeon,
    In the round-tower of my heart.

And there will I keep you forever,
    Yes, forever and a day,
Till the walls shall crumble to ruin,
    And moulder in dust away!"
              --Henry Wadsworth Longfellow

What a loving way to show children the joys of being together as a family. Another one of Longfellow's poems is **"The Village Blacksmith."** Children in the early days, as their homes and farms were established, were very familiar with the blacksmith who repaired their machinery and shoed their horses.

THE VILLAGE BLACKSMITH
"Under a spreading chestnut tree
    The village smithy stands;

The smith, a mighty man is he,
> With large and sinewy hands;
And the muscles of his brawny arms
> Are strong as iron bands.

His hair is crisp, and black, and long,
> His face is like the tan;
His brow is wet with honest sweat,
> He earns what e'er he can,
And looks the whole world in the face,
> For he owes not any man.

Week in, week out, from morn till night,
> You can hear his bellows blow;
You can hear him swing his heavy sledge,
> With measured beat and slow,
Like a sexton ringing the village bell,
> When the evening sun is low.

And children coming home from school
> Look in at the open door;
They love to see the flaming forge,
> And hear the bellows roar,
And catch the burning sparks that fly
> Like chaff from a threshing floor. . . . ."
>> --Henry Wadsworth Longfellow

    Robert Louis Stevenson was another favorite author of children. He wrote an entire book, **"A Child's Garden of Verses"** to the delight of young children everywhere.

Teachers would be remiss if we failed to quote and emphasize his poems such as samplings of the following:

MY SHADOW:
"I have a little shadow that goes in and out with me,
And what can be the use of him is more than I can see…"

THE WIND:
"I saw you toss the kites on high and blow the birds about the sky…
O wind, a-blowing all day long, O wind, that sings so loud a song!"

A GOOD BOY:
"I woke before the morning, I was happy all the day. I never said an ugly word, but smiled and stuck to play…"

WHERE GO THE BOATS?
"Dark brown is the river, Golden is the sand. It flows along forever, With trees on either hand…"

BED IN SUMMER:
In winter I get up at night, and dress by yellow candlelight. In summer, quite the other way. I have to go to bed by day…"

Spelling

Each day in Spelling, we were given a list of words to learn to spell. Most were easy for me to spell. During class the teacher pronounced each new word and we had to write it from memory. Occasionally, we had spelling bees which were fun. In a spelling bee, the whole group stood up and spelled words pronounced by the teacher when it was their turn to spell. If they missed a word, they were required to sit down. The goal was to see how long you could spell words and remain standing without having to sit down. The last student standing was the winner of the spelling bee.

When I was in the sixth grade, I competed in a Hitchcock County Spelling Contest and received a certificate from the Omaha World Herald newspaper.

Penmanship

Penmanship was emphasized when I was a child. The entire classroom practiced Penmanship at the same time. We were taught the Palmer method. We began the year learning to sit up straight and making "ovals" and "push pulls" to loosen our arm movements and to loosen our grip on the pen. Then, we learned how to make each letter correctly. Above the blackboard were the penmanship cards showing how to correctly make each letter as a capital or small letter. After we learned how to make each letter, we began learning how to correctly write words and sentences. The older students used straight pens with a pen point. We dipped the pen into our ink well or our bottle of ink. The large desks had an ink well built into the top of the desk. When it was very cold in the winter, our ink froze at night. We had blotters to take up excessive ink.

Geography

Following the afternoon recess, we had Geography every day except Friday when we had art. I enjoyed geography because it was a favorite subject of my father. Dad had to take tests to work on the railroad. It was important that he know where each town and state were located. He had a perfect score in the geography test which was a great honor for him.

One year we studied the geography of the United States. This included learning where each of the 48 states was located and the name of each state's capitol. We took drawings of the United States and filled in the name of each state and its capitol. We studied the various industries and where different crops were grown. We studied the mountains and the rivers and lakes. We learned how new inventions helped the farming and manufacturing industries.

The next year we studied the geography of the rest of the world, again learning the names of the other countries and where they were located. We studied the continents and the oceans and lakes. We learned the names of world capitols and important aspects of each country. We learned directions on a map and how to find places on a globe.

Art Class

Friday after the last recess, we had art class. Often, we made things typical of the month and its holidays. Teachers had magazines that they subscribed to that had patterns to trace around or to make copies by using carbon paper. The number of copies depended on how many were in the class. There was no other way to make copies in our country school.

When school opened in September, we often made pictures of our state flower, the Goldenrod. In October, we used patterns to make all kinds of Jack O' Lanterns and witches, black cats, bats, and ghosts. November found us making Pilgrims and turkeys and other things for Thanksgiving to decorate the school room.

In December, we decorated the school room for Christmas with Christmas trees, Christmas bells, Santas, holly, and other decorations. We had a Christmas program for our parents. I liked being a teacher's helper. I liked helping decorate and work with the Christmas program. I sat at my desk and copied off the parts for the program. We learned our speaking parts for plays, our individual recitations, and sang Christmas songs. Programs both emphasized the story of Jesus' birth and told about Santa Claus. In addition to the Christmas carols, we liked to sing "Jingle Bells," "Up on the Housetop" and "Jolly Old St. Nicholas." At the close of the program, John Wyss or Andrew Hawkinson would come in the schoolhouse door with a "Ho, Ho, Ho" dressed as Santa Claus to deliver the gifts we had exchanged and to give us a sack of candy. The schoolhouse was lit by lanterns that the fathers brought from home.

In February we made silhouettes of George Washington and Abraham Lincoln. Our main artwork though was making all kinds of valentines to give to each other. We learned to make double valentines to put a verse inside, and learned to make cupids, and arrows, and we cut pictures from wallpaper, flower catalogs, and magazines. We used ruffled crepe paper to put around the edges. We gave several to our teacher and each person in the school. The teacher made a beautifully decorated box for us to place our valentines.

During the spring months, we made spring flowers and May baskets to give to family and friends. May baskets were made out of construction paper and decorated with pretty designs or flowers. Then, they were folded to make a basket and had a handle for carrying. On May Day (May 1st), we filled them with flowers or candy. We took them to the home we wanted to give the basket to, knocked on the door, and quickly ran away so we could not be caught. If you were caught, they were supposed to kiss you!

The school year was usually uneventful. On occasion, it was disrupted by storms. I remember the time when a big blizzard came up one morning while we were in school. Uncle Ivan (Ruggles) who lived only ¼ mile west of the schoolhouse, walked through the storm to take his son, Dale, home. He also took my sister, Edna, and me to their home. It was a couple of days before Dad could come after us on a tractor with lugs. When I was a child, tractors had metal lugs on wheels instead of rubber tires. That was the only way to get through the big drifts of snow.

The only vacation during the school year was one week at Christmas. I can remember school being held one Thanksgiving Day when my parents came to school and got us at noon so we could join the family Thanksgiving dinner. The men were often husking corn about that time so school remained in session. In later years, we got one day off for Thanksgiving.

We did not have many toys to play with but we did not seem to mind. No one in the 1920's and 1930's had many toys. We learned to make things for play. At school we girls would make a hopscotch design on the bare ground behind the schoolhouse so we could play hopscotch during recesses and after noon lunch. We also played "skip the rope." Two girls would turn the rope. One at a time, we would have to run in without being caught and do all the patterns we knew about. Sometimes on warm days, we would find old boards on the school ground and build an enclosure. We stuffed the cracks with dried grass. We could climb inside and be all by ourselves. The only playground equipment on the school grounds were a couple of teeter-totters.

The boys played catch with a ball and other games they made up. There was no ball equipment so they used a piece of board for a bat and often one of the boys would bring a ball from home.

Sometimes all of the girls and boys played together—games like "Fox and Goose" in the winter after it snowed or we would build a snow fort and throw snowballs. We also played "Andy-Over" throwing the ball over the schoolhouse for the other side to catch. If they caught it, they got to change sides. We all also played "Red-Rover, Red Rover." One side would try to break the chain of hands held tightly together on the other side.

At that time, there were no immunizations so everyone got the chicken pox, red and German measles, mumps, and whooping cough. I always seemed to get every disease harder than my brother and sisters. They could be in bed a day or two, but I would be so sick for two weeks with diseases like the red measles and mumps. I had whooping cough when I was a small baby. It was hard on me, and Mother and Dad were concerned as my body was racked with incessant coughing and vomiting.

Dental care was limited. We only went to the dentist if we needed a filling or a tooth pulled. Because of very little dental care, teeth did not last into old age. Most of the older adults had their teeth pulled and wore dentures (called false teeth). Dentures caused a lot of problems as they did not fit very well.

It could get very cold walking the mile to and from school each day in the winter. So, we wore long underwear and long cotton stockings to keep warm. Even then, our feet got extremely cold. Girls did not have warm slacks to wear and our thin cotton dresses were not very warm.

There was one thing I really liked as we walked to school in the springtime and that was listening to the Western Meadowlarks. They were our state bird and their crisp, clear songs of five notes just split the air.

Eighth Grade Graduation

During the seventh and eighth grades we studied hard for the county exams that we had to pass before we could graduate from eighth grade. Not only did we go over the material in our schoolbooks, but we studied books of exam questions used in previous years. We could begin taking the tests in seventh grade and get as many subjects out of the way as possible. That way, if we did not pass a subject, we could retake it the next year.

We were required to take examinations in 14 subjects. We had no idea what would be asked in the exams so the grade did not always reflect our ability. It may have been that we had never studied that subject matter. Nevertheless, I felt I did well in the tests. We went to Trenton to take the exams in the Hitchcock County Courthouse. It was a frightening experience for us who attended rural schools. My grades were as follows:

Geography	96
History	98
Bookkeeping	95
Mental Arithmetic	98
Arithmetic	89
Grammar	91
English Composition	85
Physiology	93
Spelling	89
Penmanship	84
Drawing	90
Civics	80
Agriculture	90
Reading	83

I graduated from 8th grade on May 28, 1937. I was fourth highest in Hitchcock County in my test scores. I was presented an "Award of Honor."

We had a graduation program in the high school building in Trenton. As part of the program I played "Orange Blossom Waltz" on the piano. After the program, our family drove to Stratton where we stopped at my Grandpa and Grandma Millers. I remember how proud my Grandfather was when I told him of being fourth highest in the entire county.

Family Life At Home

On school days after we got up and were dressed, we girls set the table for breakfast and packed our school lunches. We ate breakfast together as a family, as we did every meal. Our breakfast often consisted of fried eggs and cooked cereal. When money was not plentiful, Dad ground wheat in the feed grinder to cook for cereal. I really did not like wheat mush. Cold cereal from the store was such a treat in later years.

After breakfast the whole family went to the dining room for family devotions. After Mother or Dad read from the Bible, we all kneeled at our chairs for prayer. Family devotions were never missed. Following this, before we could leave for school, our work must be done. Two of us girls washed and wiped the dishes while the third one swept the floors and dusted and made the beds. It was only then that we were ready to walk the mile to school. If it was raining hard or the weather was too snowy and cold in winter, Dad would drive us to school, but we nearly always walked home since Dad was working in town and had the car.

Windmills pumped all the water we used in the house, in the yard, and for any livestock we might have. The wind blew the windmill wheel to make it pump up water from the well. We also had a windmill in the pasture that pumped water for the cattle.

In 1924, the year I was born, things cost so much less than today:

Bread:......................$0.09/loaf
Car: $265
Milk:....................$0.53/gallon
Gas: $0.21/gallon
Postage Stamp:...............$0.02
House:..........................$7,720
Average Income:...... $1,244/yr

When I was about two years old, Dad was not feeling well. He had heart trouble, probably as a result of having the flu soon after he was married. At this time, his tonsils were badly infected and the doctor thought the constant drainage was adding to the problem. So, Dad had his tonsils removed in Dr. Bonnell's office in Trenton. We did not have specialists in those days to do surgery. Dad almost died from the local anesthetic because he was so sensitive to it. Dr. Bonnell's office did not look like today's doctor's offices. Our family spent that night with Elsie Glaser in Trenton so that Dad could be near the doctor. Elsie Glaser worked the telephone switchboard in Trenton and lived in the telephone building so she could handle calls 24 hours a day. She was a friend of my parents and was active in the Church of God in Trenton where we attended church.

Later, she moved to Stratton and was telephone operator there. Again, she lived in the telephone office. Sometimes when we were in town on a Saturday afternoon, we would go to visit her. I always thought it looked so special to be the one who sat in the telephone operator's chair and answered the calls. I loved watching her plug in the telephone cable to the line ringing in as she said, "Number Please" and then plugged the adjoining cable into the line that was being called. That looked like a lot of fun to do. She could cook and sleep and do all of her work as she listened for every call that went from one line to another. Most of the daytime she had to be at the switchboard because that was when people were calling.

Telephone

Our telephone number was 7F12, which meant we were on line 7 and our ring was one long ring followed by two short ones. Each family on our telephone line had

Early Telephone Office

a different number of rings. We could call other families on our own line by ringing their number of rings, but calls that went to a different line had to go through the telephone operator. In case of an emergency like a fire, a tornado sighting, or a death, we would ring a lot of rings in a series to alert all the people in our neighborhood. After we would hear many receivers go up, we knew the neighbors were on the line and we would give our message to everyone at once.

There was not much outside entertainment on the farm so, as we got older, we would listen in on other people's conversations on the telephone--that was why it was called a "party line!"

Early Automobiles

The Model T Ford was produced by Henry Ford's Ford Motor Company from September 1908 to October 1927. It was built in Detroit, Michigan. The year 1908 was the historic year that the automobile became popular. It was still popular in 1924 when I was born.

The Model T was built with its steering wheel on the left. Soon all the other companies copied the design. The entire engine and transmission were enclosed; the four cylinders were cast in a solid block; the suspension used two semi-elliptic springs. The car was very simple to drive, and easy and cheap to repair. A crank on the front of the car was used to start the car.

The Model T was generally regarded as the first affordable automobile that opened travel to middle-class America. It was also the first automobile mass produced on a moving assembly line with completely interchangeable parts.

The windshield on early cars was straight up and

down. The wiper came down from the top. It was only on the driver's side and operated by hand.

Henry Ford said, "I will build a car for the great multitude. It will be large enough for the family, but small enough for the individual to run and care for. It will be constructed of the best materials, by the best

Our Early Car (Fern, Dad, Verna, Edna)

men to be hired, after the simplest designs that modern engineering can devise. But it will be so low in price that no man making a good salary will be unable to own one—and enjoy with his family the blessing of hours of pleasure in God's great open spaces."

By 1918, half of all cars in America were Model T's. However, it was a monolithic black; as Ford wrote, "Any customer can have a car painted any color that he wants so long as it is black." In 1908, the price was $825. The price fell every year so that by the 1920's, the price had been reduced to $260. A majority of American drivers had learned to drive on the Model T.

By the time the Model A, (the successor to the Model T) was produced, it had a starter inside the car. If the starter did not work, the driver could still start the car with a crank.

My parents were married in 1918 and I am quite sure their first car, (before I was born) was a Model T. By 1930, they were driving a Model A car, black, with a trunk on the back. This is the car I remember as a small child. Henry Ford also built the coupe that had a Rumble Seat on the back. I remember riding in the rumble seat; that was a special experience. Dad drove Ford cars during all of my early life. My Grandfather Miller loved the Ford cars and bought new cars often. He enjoyed taking good care of their motors and always kept them spotlessly clean.

Early Lighting

We grew up, as small children, using kerosene lamps for light. They were carried from room to room. For a time we had a gas lamp, but I was frightened to use it because air had to be pumped into the gas. Only Dad lit the gas lamp. It did have a whiter, brighter light. A lamp was often kept lit, turned low, in the hallway at night so we could see if we needed to get up or if we were sick. Our bedroom doors were always left open.

Eventually, someone invented windchargers. Many of the neighbors bought 6-volt windchargers but Dad wanted more light so he put up a 32-volt windcharger. The chargers made electricity when the wind blew—the harder the wind, the more electricity. We had about 20 batteries in the basement to store the electricity when it was made. We tried to use an electric refrigerator but we did not always have enough power to keep food cold. We also tried to use an electric iron so we would not have to use the "sad irons" (that is what they were called) we heated on top of the stove burners.

The windcharger was put up north of the house. It was about the size of our windmill. With our windows

Edna, Dad, and Fern at our Farm Home with Windmill

open at night to get cool air, it made noise as it ran but we got used to it. Often a mockingbird would sit on the top of it at night and sing all night long.

When we were children, we used an icebox to keep food cold. We kept the icebox in the basement where it was cooler and the ice would last longer. We made many trips to the basement during the day for food, but we only kept things in the icebox like meat and milk. We had to keep a chunk of ice in the icebox at all times in the summer.

The last thing we would do when we went to town was to drive to the power plant where they made ice.

They would saw off a chunk of ice, the size depending on how much we wanted. We usually asked for 25 or 35 cents worth. That was the right size to fit into the ice compartment of the icebox. We wrapped it in a blanket in the trunk to keep it as cold as possible and prevent it from melting on the way home. When we got home, the first thing we had to do was carry the ice to the basement. It was heavy for us children to carry. We had to carry many heavy things in our growing up years and do whatever needed to be done.

If we wanted to make ice cream on Sunday after church, we needed to buy two chunks of ice. We kept the second chunk on the basement floor covered with blankets and rugs. We chipped off pieces of ice with an ice pick, put them in a gunny sack, and broke them into smaller pieces by hitting them with a large hammer. Our neighbor took a quart of thick cream to church for us when we were planning to make ice cream that Sunday afternoon. Mother paid her 50 cents for a quart of thick cream. Mother often made fruit ice cream with peaches, strawberries, pineapple or bananas. We ate most of the ice cream as we sat around the house on a Sunday afternoon. We liked to eat soda crackers with the ice cream. What was left would melt in the can during the night even though we kept it in the cold ice water. We children loved to hurry out of bed the next morning to drink the melted ice cream. It made a wonderful milkshake.

In the 1930's or 1940's, REA (Rural Electric Association) came to rural Nebraska. Finally, we could use all the electricity we wanted. The windcharger had its limitations. How wonderful to have an electric iron, electric range, electric refrigerator, and all the other appliances. Before this we had put a deep freezer in the shop in town so we could freeze meats and vegetables. Now we could have our freezer in the basement of our home.

Work during the week was usually scheduled on certain days of the week. Washing was always done on Monday. The water was heated in a large boiler on the kitchen range and carried to the Maytag washer. In addition, there was always a reservoir of warm water at the end of the range. Mother made soap from tallow (lard) and lye for washing clothes and dishes. Lard was cooked down from fat when they butchered.

In the summer I would often hear Mother starting the washing machine before I was out of bed. She liked to get the washing done before it was too hot. The washed clothes were run through a wringer on the washing machine into a large tub of rinse water. Then, they were put through the wringer again into a clothes basket. We girls hung the clothes outside on the clothesline, brought them in, and folded them. In winter the clothes were hung in the basement to dry.

Ironing was done on Tuesday—an all day job, after the clothes had been dampened, usually the night before, so the wrinkles would iron out easier. The shirt collars and cuffs were starched, as were other items.

We ironed with flat irons. We placed three of them on the range or on a burner of the gas stove and took turns using them. It was difficult getting them to be just the right temperature. If they were too hot, we scorched what we ironed; if too cool, they did not iron well. We would have to change irons two or three times to iron each large garment. Most everything needed to be ironed when we were young. We ironed petticoats, anklets, pillow cases, our special sheets, special dish towels, hand towels, and all of our clothes. We even ironed the overalls and work shirts. Sometimes it took more than one day to do all the ironing for a family of six. It was a real help when we later got a gas iron, though I was a bit fearful of using it.

We entertained ourselves in the winter playing marbles on the living room rug, jacks on the bare floors, or making a bingo game to play. Often, a blanket draped over a chair became a dollhouse for our dolls. The Christmas gift that I remember as the most special as a child was a cardboard playhouse with windows that opened out and a door that opened. The sides and roof were held together by glued tape. My older sister, Edna, also got a dollhouse, so sometimes we would put them together on the lawn and make a two-room playhouse. I played with my doll throughout my childhood. Earlier, we had been given a lifelike baby doll that cried and opened its eyes. We also got a wagon to play with.

Sometimes in winter, Maurice, Verna and I would go to a place in the creek where ice had formed from a spring. We skated on it, using our shoes for skates. It was fun. It did not take expensive ice skates or toys for us to share the joy of doing things together.

As we grew older, we would use free time in the summer embroidering pillow cases, dresser scarves, or tea towels. I had a lot of things in my cedar chest by the time I was married. We also spent a lot of time at the piano practicing our piano lessons.

Saturdays

Saturday morning we girls were responsible for cleaning the house. As one did the dishes and cleaned the kitchen, another cleaned the living room and dining room—that meant sweeping, dusting everything, including the baseboards, and the third sister cleaned the bedrooms and bathroom. The house was spotless when we were finished.

While we girls did the cleaning, Mother baked bread, rolls, cinnamon rolls, and pies. I especially liked her cinnamon rolls, they had so much sugar and cream on the bottom. She poured thick cream over them before she baked them.

Dad did not always have milk cows, but when he did, there was cream to churn into butter. Churning butter was another Saturday morning job. Sometimes, the butter came quickly, other times we churned and churned before we began seeing the little flecks of butter and finally the butter all separated from the buttermilk. Then we needed to wash the butter several times to get all the buttermilk out, work the water out with the butter paddle and finally, it was molded into a round shape and put away for use. Mother also made cottage cheese from milk that was heated on the back of the range until it clabbered and turned to cottage cheese. We put it in the colander to drain away the whey. Her cottage cheese tasted so good; it was a real treat.

When we went to town on Saturdays, we always went to Grosse's to buy our groceries. When Mother raised chickens, she saved any extra eggs and took them to the store to sell. What she got for the eggs was used to help purchase what we needed at the store.

Dad raised a large patch of watermelons. In the fall, he took watermelons by the trunk full to the store to sell. They were large melons, and I think they sold for 25 cents to 50 cents each.

When baths were taken in the summer, we heated water over the stove and carried it to the bathtub. But the bathroom was too cold for a bath in the winter so we took sponge baths in a basin by the stove in the dining room. The bathroom did not have heat during that time.

We lived in the kitchen and dining room during the cold months of winter. The sliding doors to the living room were drawn shut. Later on, the coal furnace was replaced with a propane stove in the dining room. The range heated the kitchen. The bedrooms were cold in winter. They had no storm windows. We slept between cotton blankets. Even then sometimes Mother would warm a blanket and lay it in the bed just before we jumped into bed. Once in bed, I curled up in my flannel nightgown, and I did not move before morning.

After lunch on Saturday, we all went to town. Mother took what little inheritance money she got from her parents' estate to give all of us girls piano lessons. We studied with Mrs. Wade Martin, our banker's wife. Edna and I had half-hour lessons. Mother had an hour lesson. She had always wanted to play the piano well. She was one of Mrs. Martin's best students. I remember her playing "Robin's Return" at a recital. Verna May, who Mother did not think was yet old enough for lessons, began to play our pieces by ear. So, Mrs. Martin took her on part of Mother's time. Verna was the one who became the musician in the family, going on to win recognition in music, getting her degrees in music, and teaching piano at the college level.

We all played in the recitals each year. We each played piano solos. Sometimes Edna and I played duets and all four of us (Mother, Edna, Verna and I) would play together on two pianos.

After our piano lessons, we girls would go down to see Grandma Miller while Mother took her lesson.

Grandpa and Grandma Miller were an important part of my life. They had retired early from the homestead east of our farm and moved to town, where they owned a large home on a corner lot with a big yard. Grandpa loved new cars. He traded cars often. I remember his cars were almost like new when he traded them in because he took such good care of them. As a child, I would see him cleaning any dirt or erosion off the battery and motor. Grandma said when Grandpa was downtown a lot, she knew he would be coming home with a new Ford car! Ford cars were the only cars Grandpa would buy. Grandpa did all the driving, which was mostly to Trenton to church or to the farms of his family. Grandma always rode in the back seat. Once when they came to visit us, Grandpa just loved the fragrance of Mother's regal lilies. So Mother gave him a bouquet to take home. He announced he would put them in his bedroom that night so he could enjoy their fragrance all night—but he admitted he had to take them to the dining room because their fragrance was too strong.

MY *Life* ON THE *Prairie* FERN MILLER NILSON

We liked going to their house on Saturdays. Grandma always made us feel welcome. She was a heavy set woman with her hair pulled back tightly into a knot. The skirts of her dresses reached her shoes. We often sat in the sunroom off the kitchen and just talked while she mended or darned. In the summer we sat in the swing on the porch.

Grandma made orange bread that was really special. She would knead and knead the dough and make it into round loaves. In the summer I loved to eat the red currants that I picked from bushes in their yard. There was a large cherry tree in the yard, too. I can still see Grandma sitting on a couch on the back porch and pitting cherries for pies.

The range was the center of the kitchen. We used it for cooking and heating. It had several burners for cooking and a large reservoir at the end that heated water for washing clothes, baths, and other needs. Above the cooking surface were two warming ovens that would keep food warm. The oven was below the cooking area. Sometimes in the winter, we would keep a pan of water warm with sassafras bark. The family liked sassafras tea.

When I was small, we had a pump on the right side of the kitchen sink. We pumped what water we needed for washing and cooking. Later, my father put in a water pressure tank in the basement. Water was pumped into it by the windmill. Then air was pumped in to make pressure when we turned on the faucets on all the fixtures. That was another great improvement just as the electricity and stove and refrigerator were.

Under the counter were two large bins that held

50 pounds of flour and sugar. The flour and sugar sacks were washed and bleached to make dresses and kitchen towels.

Under the sugar bin was a bread drawer. Mother baked enough loaves on Saturday to last most of the week for lunches and meals. In one corner above the counter was a "cool cupboard." It had a square opening to the outside that kept food cold in winter—and somewhat cooler in the spring and fall when the temperatures were cooler. Nothing was refrigerated in the icebox in the summer except meat and milk. We could also set foods on the sun porch that was screened in since it was very cold in winter.

One other special treat was pickled herring. It was a Swedish dish. We did not prepare many Swedish dishes, but we liked it when the folks would buy a keg of herring. It had been put in salt water brine to keep it from spoiling as it was shipped overseas to America. The brine had to be soaked out in fresh water. Then it was cut into chunks and prepared with water, vinegar, onions, sugar, and spices. We snacked on it during the day.

When it snowed, my father would keep his eyes open for a snow-covered thistle. Often there would be a rabbit hiding in the thistle. Dad carried his gun at such times and would shoot a rabbit for our supper. It tasted so good.

Sometimes, he would shoot ducks and geese when they were in the area They would land in the fields to eat corn that was left on the ground after harvest. In the summer when we had a big rain, ponds in a low place in the south and north fields held water. It seemed they had no longer formed when the frogs started croaking. They made a lot of noise. We could hear them at the house. We could also hear coyotes at night howling in the fields and sometimes close to the buildings.

Our early cars were cold in the winter because they had no heater. We covered our legs and feet with blankets and wore warm outer clothes. In the summer we opened the car windows to try to get cooler air, if possible.

We children went to high school in Stratton when we graduated from eighth grade in the country school. Also, my Father had his manufacturing business in town, so my parents decided we should go to church there as well. A group organized a new church using an empty Christian Church building. They called the new church the Christian Union Church. There was one heating stove in the center of the church. Sunday School classes met in different parts of the room. When we were small we had a church Christmas program. We also had a Children's Day program on Children's Day, which was in early June. We had special clothes to wear on Sunday—good dresses and coats and Sunday shoes. Saturday evening, my father would polish all the shoes so they would look nice for church. We always wore our best for God.

My parents were involved in the planting of this church. My father was on the church board many years. My mother was Sunday School Superintendent and teacher of the Adult Sunday School class for a time. My sister, Verna, often played the piano for church services.

Early Christmases

Christmases were special. Our first Christmas tree was a small artificial tree. It was kept in the top kitchen cupboard. It was only 3-4 feet tall. We decorated it with real candles that were placed in holders on the tree. As I grew older, we began to buy an evergreen tree at the store. I loved the smell of the evergreen and what fun it was to decorate it with glass balls and icicles. After electricity came, we added strings of electric lights.

On one Saturday in December we would drive the 35 miles to McCook to do our Christmas shopping. My father gave each of us children a dollar to spend. If Edna and I put our money together, we had 50 cents to spend on each member of the family. I can remember getting Dad a billfold for 50 cents and a casserole dish for Mother for about 39 cents. About this time, Kleenex came into the stores for the first time, colored tissues in gift boxes with powder puffs. These became a special gift for Edna and me to give to each other. Before this, we had only handkerchiefs to carry with us; they added to the washing and ironing.

The wrapping paper and ribbons were saved from Christmas packages and used year after year. It always seemed as pretty as the year before. We did not get a lot of gifts during the depression, but we always received at least one gift. When I later went to high school, the gift I most wanted for Christmas from Mother and Dad was an inexpensive Timex watch. The rest of the students seemed to have watches and I wanted to have one, too.

Christmas Eve came that year, and my package was the watch I wanted. How thrilled I was.

We always had our Christmas dinner on Christmas Eve and opened our gifts after we ate. We often went to our grandparents home for Christmas dinner. Frequently, they gave us fancy handkerchiefs for gifts. One year Grandpa gave each of us grandchildren a silver dollar. These gifts were just as special as the more expensive gifts we bought in later years.

Michigan

Mother had come to Nebraska from Michigan. Her family was still in Michigan and Ohio, so many summers in the 1920's and 1930's we would go there for several weeks to visit. How excited I was to go. I never could understand why Mother dreaded the trip. I did not realize she had to handle four small children, our food, and the luggage when we changed train stations in Chicago.

Most of the time we went to Michigan by train because my father could not get away in the summer due to his business and farm work. We rode in the Pullman cars on the passenger train. How exciting it was to have the porters come and make up our beds. My Mother and my younger brother and sister slept in the lower berth. Edna and I slept in the upper berth.

Because the trip took several days by train, we needed to carry food that would keep without refrigeration. We mostly took dried beef sandwiches, cookies, and fruit to eat. The trains were not air conditioned, so the windows were open. Unfortunately, the open windows not only let in the wind, but the smoke and soot from the engine. The countryside seemed to fairly "fly by" as we gathered speed. I thought the conductors had such an important job as they checked our tickets and took on new passengers at towns along the way. The call of "All Aboard" meant we would soon be on our way again.

Mother had packed our clothes in a large black trunk that we put in the baggage car on the train. We also packed some things in suitcases that we carried with us.

In Chicago, porters called "Redcaps" met the train and carried our bags for 5¢ each. They helped us to a taxi that took us to another station. Here we boarded another train for Michigan. Again, the redcaps took our luggage and put it on the train.

Mother's family lived near Litchfield, Michigan. When I was small, both of her parents were living. My grandparents lived in a large house in the country. We always slept upstairs in one of the three bedrooms. Behind the house was a large two-story barn. The hay and feed were kept on the upper floor that had an incline so they could drive into it. As children, we loved to play in the haymow. The dairy cows were kept below on the lower floor. In the early morning I would awaken to hear them bringing the cows in to be milked. The cows were kept in a pasture across the railroad tracks that ran on the west side of the buildings. They were driven down the railroad tracks, then on the road south of the house, and then down the lane to the barn. Soon, I could hear the separator going in the separator room downstairs so I knew the milking was done. The separator separated the milk from the cream. My grandparents sold the cream. They also sold eggs that we girls helped gather in the afternoon.

There was a large cement porch on the east side of the kitchen with a pump where my grandparents pumped their water. And there was a big woodshed on the back end of the house where they stored wood for winter and other things.

East of the house was a two-story tenant house. At first Aunt Verna's family lived there and helped with the farming and cattle. Later, Aunt Verna and her children, Donald and Anna, moved into my grandparent's house to care for them and do the farm work. Between the two houses was a huge garden. I liked to pick off large rhubarb leaves, with the stalks, to use as an umbrella.

We children loved to explore their woods. Usually we drove a horse hitched to a cart to go down the lane leading to the woods, and we liked to walk along the railroad tracks to pick wild strawberries. The roads were graveled and lined with large trees, ferns, and corn lilies. Sometimes we girls walked down the road to play with the Lockwood children on a nearby farm.

Aunt Verna (my Mother's sister) would take my grandparents and us to Columbus, Ohio, to visit Aunt May, Mother's sister. Aunt May lived in a big house in a suburb. Uncle Ed had an electrical shop in the city.

Occasionally, my father went with us to Michigan for a short visit—or he came to get us. The trip by car took at least three days, perhaps more. The roads were gravel and narrow and winding around hills and rivers.

The gravel roads were dusty and often had a big ridge of gravel in the middle of the road. These ridges had to be crossed if we went around a slow vehicle. That would make the car swing as we crossed them. We only averaged about 35 miles per hour, which was the speed limit at that time. Sometimes we did not even get to Iowa the first day on our trip. It was a hot trip in the summer with no air conditioning and the dust just fogged behind each car. It was easier driving if we came on a few miles of pavement near a large city.

New Transportation

An exciting new train was built—a streamlined train, all silver, called the Denver Zephyr was to run on our Burlington (CB&Q) Railroad from Denver to Chicago. It was scheduled to make its maiden trip on our railroad. We heard it would be going very fast. We drove to the railroad crossing north of our farm the day it was to make its first run. There were people at every crossing all along the way to see the new wonder. As a child, I could not imagine how fast it would be going—I wondered if it would go so fast that I would miss it! As the whistle sounded, we knew it was coming and there it was—so shiny and new and streamlined, not belching black smoke like the other trains.

As the Zephyr began its regular runs, we would stand in our farmyard and watch it go through Stratton every evening about 7:05 p.m. We could see Stratton and the Republican river through a break in the hills.

Airplanes were rare. If we heard one, we would strain our eyes until we could locate it in the sky. Once a small plane came to McCook. People could take rides. We went down and Dad took us up in the plane. I remember how people looked like ants on the ground. What an experience for a child! The next trip up, the plane crashed but I do not remember anyone being seriously hurt.

Invention Of Grain Bin On Combine

In wheat harvest, early header and reel pushed by horses (below) Steam engine that Dad used to thresh grain.

MY *Life* ON THE *Prairie*   FERN MILLER NILSON

After Dad and Mother were married, Dad raised wheat on the farm. One year they had a fire in the wheat field that was started from the exhaust on the old International tractor. The fire destroyed 20 acres of their wheat and also burned north across the road into the neighbor's field.

At first, Dad used a "header" for harvesting wheat. Bundles of grain

Dad and his invention of the Grain Bins on Early Combines.

were threshed by a threshing machine run by a steam engine. This was hot, hard work in the middle of summer. Later, Dad bought a combine and used "baggers" one season. The next year, he put a wagon beside the combine instead of the baggers. The third year, Dad put a grain bin on the combine. He also put an extension elevator on the combine to run the grain into the bin on the combine. Many people came to see Dad's invention and fixed their combines the same way. About 1921, Dad wrote to the International Harvester Company showing them the extension elevator and the bin for grain. He sent them a picture of it. The next year International Harvester came out with it, as did the other manufacturers of combines. Dad never received any compensation for his invention. If he had taken out a patent on his invention before telling the other companies, he might have profited very well financially.

In 1926, my father's brother (Roy Miller) and his wife (Ellen Miller) rented the farm during the farming season. They lived in the south end of the machine shed where Mother and Dad had built living quarters. The crops were a failure that year due to drought and a devastating hail storm on Labor Day. The hail storm destroyed everything in the fields and yard. All the leaves were stripped from the trees, and the buildings were damaged.

The Miller Wonder Feed Mill

My father was busy in 1926 manufacturing the Miller Wonder Feed Mill he had invented. He took out a patent on the feed mill and established Miller Manufacturing Company. He first began his business in Trenton, Nebraska where Carl, his oldest brother, lived at that time. After a few months in Trenton, Dad moved his business to Stratton, Nebraska.

Dad's first shop was in a building owned by C. U. Lionberger, on the west side of the Lionberger Lumber Yard. Next, he rented a building from the McCook Building and Loan Association because this building provided more room. But he encountered problems with this building as the McCook Building and Loan Association did not maintain the building.

The Miller Wonder Feed Mill Dad's Second Invention

My Father Builds His Shop

In 1934, my father decided to build his own shop. It was built of cement blocks and extended halfway back to the alley and was located just north of the Craw Implement Company. This building was used the entire time Dad was in business. My father sold his feed mills in every state of the United States except Delaware. Many were sold in Canada. Miller Wonder Feed Mills were also sold through Link Mfg. Co. in Fargo, North Dakota. This company was a distributor who sold to dealers in the United States and Canada. Machines sold to Link Mfg. Co. had their name on the Feed Mill that said, "Made for Link Mfg. Co., Fargo, N.D." in smaller print.

All the feed mills, or feed grinders as we often called them, were taken to the depot at Stratton and shipped out by train. The steel and other needed supplies were also shipped in by train. After he moved into town from the farm, Grandpa Miller often walked to Dad's shop from his home, one and one-half blocks north, to help assemble the feed mills for Dad. They sold for $48.50. Dad made the Miller Wonder Feed Mills until about 1945 when he devoted all his manufacturing time to other inventions, and especially to making the Miller Discs. By this time, the building had been expanded all the way to the alley.

The Miller Garden Weeder

Later in the 1930's, my Father invented a hoe that he called the Miller Garden Weeder. He wanted a hoe that would slice under the soil, cut off the weeds, and leave the soil in place. He sold the weeders in bundles of a dozen. One time he loaded up a trailer full of weeders and pulled it behind the car. We went north into the Ogallala, Nebraska area, stopping at dealers along the way to market the Garden Weeders.

My Father and Mother

The family had gone along to make it a little vacation. Our destination was a lake where we hoped to fish. But when we arrived, the family who lived at the lake and managed it looked like they were just getting over smallpox and a storm was approaching, so we immediately headed back toward home as night was falling. We got as far as Imperial, driving through heavy rain with whitecaps on the standing water along the roadside and in the fields. The next morning we got to Stratton and crossed the bridge over the Republican River just before it was washed out.

The library table in the living room of our home on the farm was Dad's office desk where he took care of his business. He typed up his own statements and letters using two fingers. He had perfected his own typing system because there was no one to teach him to type. I marveled at how fast he typed with just two fingers.

Corn Harvest

Later, Dad went to raising corn. For three years, 1927-1928-1929, we had big corn crops, raising thousands of bushels of corn. I remember the sounds of fall harvesting as the teams of horses and wagons left the machine shed at daybreak each morning to go to the fields to pick corn. The corn crop was harvested by hand and shucked in the field. The cornhuskers used pegs or hooks strapped to their palms to shuck the corn ears. The horses were kept in the north end of the machine shed; the men slept in the south end where the folks had built living quarters. Sometimes, they slept on beds in the basement of the house.

The wagons had a higher backboard (bang board) on the one side, and we could hear the thud of the ears of corn hitting the bang board as corn was picked and thrown up into the wagon. The horses pulling the wagons started and stopped as the men made their way down the rows. Throughout the day, we could hear the men calling to their horses to "get up" or "whoa." When the wagons were full, the husked corn was piled in huge piles to the west and northwest of the house.

Later the corn was shelled with a cornsheller run by a belt attached to the tractor pulley. The shelled corn was

Husking Corn

trucked to town, leaving behind huge piles of corn cobs. Dad sold the corn at 25-30¢ per bushel during those years when prices were very low. Sometimes the price was even lower than that, but he did not sell at the cheaper prices.

Corncobs were used for starting the fires in the range and furnace each morning. Then coal was added to provide the lasting hot heat. My father would get up early in the morning to start the fires so the stove was ready to cook breakfast and the house warm when the family got up. Some farmers burned corn for fuel during those years when it was cheaper than coal, but my father did not do that because it was against his principles.

When we needed coal, Dad drove the truck to the lumberyard in town to purchase a load of coal. The truck was then weighed and he was charged for the amount of his load. Coal was sold by the ton, and it came into Stratton by train. It was kept in coal sheds owned by the lumberyard. When Dad brought the coal home, he opened a basement window and scooped it into the fuel room in the basement. Then, there was the task of cleaning up the coal dust that filtered throughout the basement and up into the house.

Mother worked hard cooking for the cornpickers. One year she used the money that Dad gave her for cooking to buy her good set of Bavarian china. It was white with a gold band. The good china was always used when we had company. It is still in excellent condition. No pieces have been broken even though the small cups were very fragile.

Wheat Harvest

After raising corn for several years, Dad once again began raising wheat. There was more farm work in raising corn. Corn seed was planted with a two-row lister that made a furrow down to moisture, where the seed was dropped and covered with soil. When the corn plants grew 4-6 inches tall, a cultivator was used to pull the soil in around the plants. In addition, corn needed to be picked in the fall and then shelled.

Hard Red Winter wheat could be planted in

September and combined in early July of the following year. When the wheat was ripe, it needed to be combined as soon as possible to keep it from shattering and to get it into the bin before a storm could cause loss of the crop. Dad would check the hardness and ripeness of the wheat by picking off heads, threshing them in his hands, and biting down on the kernels to see if they were hard and ripe. As children, we were cautioned to not get the wheat beards in our throats as the barbs tended to pull downwards and we could not get them out of our throats. When the wheat was finally ripe, each morning again it was checked to see if it was dry. Combining could not begin until all the dampness from the dew was gone and it was perfectly dry.

As the combine cut the wheat, our truck had to meet the combine and drive up to its bin where the wheat was unloaded into the truck. While the combine was making another round, the truck was driven to our granary where the wheat was scooped into the bins in the granary. As soon as the wheat was scooped off, they drove back to the field for another load. This was kept up until all the wheat was harvested. It took many days to finish harvest.

We children spent hours riding in the back of the truck and letting the wheat fill up around our bare feet and legs. Again, it was Mother's job to have a big dinner for the harvesters. As we girls got older, we helped with the preparation of the food and dishes. In the afternoon, lunches were taken to the field—often pie and lemonade. Supper was eaten late for they worked in the fields as long as they could see and the wheat kernels stayed dry.

In the weeks that followed, Dad would climb into the

bins that were full of wheat and reach into the wheat as far as he could to be sure it was all right. If wheat had too much moisture in it, it could get hot causing combustion and fire. It was again scooped into the truck and hauled to town for money.

Some years Dad would hire custom combines to harvest the wheat. Later, he purchased another combine. My brother, Maurice, was old enough to drive the tractor and Dad drove the combine. Part of the time, I drove the truck. After the truck was full with wheat, I drove it to the elevator in town. I never felt comfortable handling the big load over the sandy road in the pasture or in driving into the elevator.

For a short time Dad tried farming by using a truck for power instead of a tractor. He thought the cab of a truck would be better than sitting on a tractor. It wasn't long before tractors were built with cabs.

Dad had the farm planted to milo maize one year. It was so dry that the crop did not develop sufficiently to harvest. Dad sold the crop in the field to George Stahley, who brought in hundreds of sheep to forage off the milo crop. Each morning we could see the flock coming over the edge of the pasture to the west, where they had spent the night. They always followed the lead sheep in a "V" formation to graze the fields during the day. When George Stahley left with his sheep, he gave Dad ten lambs to butcher. Dad butchered them one at a time that summer. We could put the meat of an entire lamb in our icebox.

The Depression Years

In 1934, during the height of the Great Depression prices were as follows:

    A loaf of bread cost a $0.10
    A quart of milk cost $0.08
    Oatmeal, 5 lb. bag, $0.20
    Butter $0.20
    Pure Lard, lb., $0.10
    Flour, standard 48 lb. sack, $1.65
    No. 1 potatoes, 15-lb.sack $0.35
    Raisins, seedless, 3 lb., $0.25
    Bacon squares, lb., $0.12
    No. 1 eggs, dozen, $0.17 ½
    Cheese, lb., $0.20
    Sugar, 10 lbs., $0.55
    Peas, can, $0.15
    Kerosene oil, gal., $0.14
    Laundry soap, 6 giant bars, $0.25
    Toilet paper, 4--1,000 sheet rolls, $0.25

One summer a few weeds (probably thistles) remained on the field after Dad had disked the field. Dad wanted it clean so he asked us children to go out with him to pull any weeds the disk missed. Later, we realized this was a huge mistake because with no cover on the ground, the dust storms carried away the topsoil. However, we children were always glad to help and work together. Dad did, however, caution us to watch for snakes under the weeds. We always grew up with a terrible fear of snakes. Dad told many frightening stories of his experiences of nearly being bitten by deadly rattlesnakes.

We always watched for snakes wherever we walked whether in the yard, the garden and orchard, or in the field. I hated the big bull snakes as much as the rattlers.

On our next trip to town after helping pull weeds, Dad took us to the drug store for an "Eskimo Pie" (ice cream bar). I had never heard of one. That was such a special treat.

Food From The Farm

Mother always planted a big garden each year and raised chickens for eating and eggs. Dad planted a big patch of sweetcorn, watermelons, muskmelons, and some pumpkins and squash in the field. We also had a large orchard of fruit trees. Much of our food came from the farm. There were some gooseberry bushes on the back side of the house. Gooseberries were very sour to eat or make into pie. We tried to find one that was turning a bit brown; it was sweeter. We also raised some rhubarb, but the family liked the orchard fruits better. Behind the chicken house was a black currant bush. It made wonderful pie, similar to huckleberries that grew in the mountains.

When it was hot and dry in the summer, Mother would connect all the hoses together and pull them from tree to tree in the orchard to water them. She would make a basin around the trees to hold the water. There were at least 40 fruit trees of many varieties.

On a summer morning, Mother would go to the

chicken pen to catch a young fryer for dinner. When it was caught, she took the butcher knife, which she had given a sharper edge by running it back and forth on the cement steps, and stepped on the feet of the chicken. After Mother killed the chicken, we poured boiling water into a bucket and dipped the chicken into the boiling water until the feathers could be pulled out easily. We picked feathers until all were gone and peeled the skin off of the feet; even the toe nails were snapped off. Then, we took a newspaper, set it on fire in the yard, and singed the chicken or singed it over a burner on the gas stove. Finally, it was ready to be cut up. This was almost a daily job in the summer to provide fresh meat for the table. On Saturday, we often cleaned an extra chicken for Sunday dinner. After we put a freezer in Dad's manufacturing shop in town, we put chicken fryers in the freezer for later use.

We had peas, beans, and many other vegetables to eat from the garden. Sometimes, we gathered a weed called "lamb's quarters" from around the buildings for greens; they tasted just like spinach and were delicious. Salt dips were placed by each plate for fresh radishes and green onions.

When the sweet corn was ready for harvest, one of us girls would be sent to the field with a very large kettle to get enough corn from the corn patch to completely fill the kettle. My father could make an entire meal on sweet corn; we all ate several ears. When corn was ready for canning, we would drive to the sweet corn patch in the field and gather corn in gunny sacks. Then, we would go back to the yard where the whole family helped clean it for drying or canning. Dad had a sharp knife and he would cut off the ends of the ears. We children took off the husks and silk and trimmed the ears of corn while Mother blanched the corn and cooled it. Then, Mother and we girls all helped cut the corn from the cobs.

Before we had freezers, Mother dried lots of the corn. Clean white sheets were placed on the roof of the chicken house where the dishpans of cut corn were spread out to dry. Frequently, we would climb up the ladder to the roof to stir it. It had to be very hard and dry before it was put into gallon jars. One year, I remember we had an infestation of army worms. One of us stayed on the roof killing any worms that tried to climb up the building to get at the corn.

Sharing the first ripe tomato from the garden was a special occasion. It would be cut into equal parts so that each one of us got our share. We would sprinkle salt on it and eat it in our hands. Everyone in the family shared the joy of these special things that we grew, especially the first one harvested from the garden.

Dad kept an eye out for the first ripe watermelon. When it sounded just right as he thumped it, he would carry it to the end of the sidewalk and slice it for us to eat. It was cut in long slices that we held in our hands. We spit the seeds on the ground. The "heart" of the melon was especially sweet. When watermelons became plentiful, we often ate only the choicest part of the melons, which were the hearts. Dad raised watermelons by the truckload. He gave many to friends who came to the farm, filling their trunks with melons. He sold watermelons to Grosse's Store. We also had an abundance of muskmelons to eat. We preferred the Rocky Ford variety.

My favorite snacks between meals were cucumber or tomato slices, salted and peppered between slices of bread to make a sandwich. The family liked cucumbers prepared with vinegar, salt and pepper. Cucumbers and tomatoes took the place of a salad. Sometimes we children made a handful of buttered soda crackers for snacks.

We seldom had candy or gum. Our "gum" was often paraffin wax that we chewed until it became soft and pliable. A half-stick or less of gum was chewed more than once. At night we would put it on the bedpost to keep for the next day! A package of gum cost five cents. Candy bars also cost five cents. When we got one, we made it last a long time.

Our fruit came from the large orchard south of the driveway. Dad especially liked the mulberries. He loved to walk from one tree to the next eating the luscious fruit. He had planted many different kinds of mulberries—black, white, pink and purple. Each variety seemed to be different in size and flavor. Mulberries were picked for dessert to be eaten with cream and sugar. If we gathered a lot of berries, we shook them onto a sheet. We made mulberry pies and mulberry jam. Many were canned for later use.

During World War II sugar was rationed. We would have to get extra sugar stamps so we could buy sugar for canning. Sometimes we had to use saccharin because we were out of sugar.

Then the cherries came on. We had a black cherry

tree in the yard; the red cherries were in the orchard. When they were first starting to ripen, I would hunt for the bird-pecked cherries; they were always the sweetest. It probably was not a good idea, but I never got sick from eating them. On hot afternoons, we girls liked to go to the orchard to pick some cherries, pit them, add sugar and water, and make a cherry drink. We would sit on the front porch swing savoring the fruit drink.

Peaches were my mother's favorite fruit—and mine. We had yellow peaches and white peaches. How I enjoyed walking from one tree to another picking ripe peaches to eat beside the tree. The white peaches were especially good—to me they seemed a luxury, and it was a delight to eat your fill.

Mother was faithful in picking up any windfall apples that fell on the ground and making them into applesauce. We canned a lot of fruit for winter use—cherries, peaches, pears, and applesauce.

My mother also watched for the pineapple to come to the store. I knew of no one else who did it, but Mother would buy a crate of pineapple each year to can.

The pineapples were sliced; then we all helped peel and take out the eyes. As we cut the pineapple away from the core into wedges to can, we would eat the cores. They were so good, but our tongues became so sore!

Not always did we have livestock, but sometimes Dad kept a cow to milk. When I was quite small, the milk was carried to a milk house that had two cement tanks of cold, running water where the milk was kept cool. When the milk was brought from the cowshed to be cooled, it was a good time to take a cup and have Dad fill it with fresh, foamy milk to drink. The water ran from one cement tank to another in the milk house, then ran into a stock tank behind the building to water any animals we might have.

When Dad did not have milk cows, we bought our milk at the store in town for 10 cents a quart. Thick cream was 20 cents a pint.

The water from the stock tank was also used for watering the garden nearby. Mother's big garden grew all the vegetables. She used a garden cultivator to make the rows for planting and to loosen the soil beside the rows of plants.

One day as she was working in the garden, she heard a splash. She turned around, saw a box pushed up to the tank, and instantly knew that my brother, Maurice, who was very small, had fallen into the tank of water. Fortunately, she could grab him out of the water and kept him from drowning. Maurice was playing in the water and had reached in too far. Sometimes, we children got into the tank of water on hot days. That was our only swimming pool. We would also play in the sprinklers on the lawn.

Autumn

Fall was a special time when the air turned crisp and the dry leaves crackled beneath our feet. I loved the sight of the full harvest moon. When frost was imminent, we would go out to the field on a cool, fall evening and gather in melons and pumpkins and squash to store in the basement for the winter days ahead.

When we grew corn, there were times that my father had corn bound into bundles. When the bundles were dry, we would make the bundles into shocks. What a lovely fall picture it made. The corn shocks later became feed for the animals.

In the winter we made Snow Ice Cream. When we had a deep, clean snow storm, we would take a pan outside, brush off the top of the snow, and fill a pan with clean snow. We took it indoors, added cream and sugar and vanilla to make the right consistency of ice cream, and dished it up in bowls to eat.

Swinging In The Elm Trees

There were two very large elm trees north of the garden and the milk house. Dad put a swing in the east one. We children, especially Edna and I, would pump ourselves up very high in the swing. Sometimes we faced each other and pumped up together, swinging out high and far. As I "pumped up" high in the swing, I would so often quote the poem,

THE SWING
How do you like to go up in the swing,
    Up in the air so blue?
Oh, I do think it the pleasantest thing
    Ever a child can do!
Up in the air and over the wall,

> Till I can see so wide,
> Rivers and trees and cattle and all
> Over the countryside—
> Till I look down on the garden green,
> Down on the roof so brown--
> Up in the air I go flying again,
> Up in the air and down!
> --Robert Louis Stevenson

When cold weather arrived, Dad would sometimes butcher a steer. He would carry a quarter of beef up to the house and lay it on a table on the back enclosed porch. It stayed almost frozen from the cold temperatures. Dad or Mother would go out and cut off steak for supper. Sometimes we even had steak for breakfast. Because there was no refrigeration, we ate a lot of whatever was available. We especially liked the liver, fried and served with raw onions. Some of the meat was cut in small chunks and canned in quart jars. We even put steak up in large jars. It was fried and then covered with melted tallow that hardened and preserved it. We took out a few pieces as it was needed. Occasionally a hog was butchered. I was delighted when someone shared some fresh pork tenderloin or ribs with us. It was so good and a real treat.

An advertisement in a 1935 paper listed these specials—

Oranges	1 cent each
Grapefruit	29 cents per dozen
Pork Roast	19 cents per pound
Beef Shoulder Roast	12 cents a pound

Bread .... 10 cents a loaf
Package Tea Rolls .... 5 cents

The clerks in the grocery stores went to the shelves to get the items we wanted and placed the groceries in sacks for us.

When we drove to McCook on a Saturday morning to do shopping, before we left for home, Mother would buy a package of tea rolls for 5 cents and some minced ham to eat in the rolls as a sandwich. We usually ate two or three apiece; they tasted so good. It was a treat.

Wild Flowers

Wild flowers in the pasture were beautiful with the coming of spring. Yucca, tall and waxy, thickly dotted the pasture. And there was the indescribable joy of going to the pasture each spring to find the wild sweetpeas that grew among the sagebrush on some of the sandy hills. Dad knew just where to find them. We would gather them by the armful. And, there were lots of cactus. The beautiful blossoms, mostly yellow, later turned to prickly pears. When a pink pin-cushion cactus was found displaying its deep pink color, we thought it was especially lovely.

And, there were brilliant-blue spider lilies, wild geraniums, and sand flowers. The wild roses were so fragrant and delicate as we buried our faces in the blossoms to breathe deeply of their sweetness. Each wild flower had its own special beauty and place in our hearts. There were also the old-fashioned pink and yellow roses north of the house that excelled in their beauty and fragrance. New rose varieties do not bear the sweetness of the roses of long ago.

Family Trips

About June, we would drive to Colorado to get red raspberries and bing cherries. The folks would buy many lugs of raspberries and cherries at roadside markets. One of our favorite things to eat was red raspberries and cream. Before we left for home, we would buy a pint of thick cream and a loaf of bread at the store and go to a city park to eat our supper.

We took many trips to the mountains in Colorado. When we were small, the mountain roads were narrow with sharp curves and were quite steep. We often stopped at mountain springs at the side of the road to put water in the radiator. Radiators would boil easily because of the steep climb and hot weather. It was dangerous to take off the radiator cap as the boiling water would shoot up into the air.

We also enjoyed stopping beside the mountain streams and gathering rocks or climbing up into the mountains where we would gather evergreen branches to take home with us. They made the car smell so good. I loved the pine and spruce trees. I would stick my head out of the car window to fill my lungs with their fragrance. I always hated to leave the cool, crisp mountain air. I would look back as long as I could see the forest and mountains. The landscape across eastern

Colorado seemed so bleak and desolate in comparison. Yet, when we reached Stratton, I thought it was the best place in the world.

In our early years when we took trips, we stayed in cabins at night. The cabins were very bare. They had a bed frame with a mattress and springs and little else. We had to furnish our bedding and anything else we might need. The cabins had no bathroom; everyone used a central facility. The cabins cost $1.00 per night; we all stayed in the one room.

One summer, Mother and Dad decided to go to a camp meeting at Grand Junction, Colorado. We were there at the time when the Colorado peaches, pears, and plums were ready. Mother and Dad took the big truck so that we could bring back a load of fruit. There were six of us in the family at that time. Dad, Mother, and the two youngest, Verna May and Maurice, rode in the cab. Edna and I rode in the back of the truck. I can still feel the wind blowing against my face and through my hair. We stood at the sides of the truck box or sat on a trunk that held our clothing and supplies. We moved freely around in the truck box. There was no protection and no seat belts!

We spent the first night on a side road near Fort Morgan, Colorado. We took two mattresses with us in the back of the truck that we slept on in the truck bed on our way to Grand Junction. Mother cooked on a small gas stove. The next morning, as we drove from Greeley to Denver, I felt the thrill of standing in the back of the truck as we seemed to fairly fly past the houses and traffic.

Some of the mountain roads were not very wide

so Dad would need to honk the truck horn as we went around sharp curves on the mountain passes, like Monarch Pass, to let traffic coming from the opposite direction know that we were coming. It was a bit scary at times to be out in the open on the mountain roads, but I knew Dad would get us there safely. Edna and I could look at those in the cab through the window in the back of the cab, or talk to the family through the side windows.

It was raining as we drove beside the Black Canyon of the Gunnison and all six of us had to climb inside the cab. Dad was concerned about the wet, slick highway. There were no protective barriers on the side of the road.

At Grand Junction, Dad had the entire truck filled with bulk fruit. Most of the load was peaches, but we also had some pears and a few plums. The two mattresses were put on top of the fruit to keep it cool. It was suggested that Edna and I ride in the narrow space at the very back of the truck box to protect us in case the load would shift. But that left us without any way to talk to the family in the cab while we were traveling.

On the way back from Grand Junction, Dad had a concern about the brakes. When we stopped, Mother would jump out of the cab and put rocks behind the wheels to keep the truck from rolling. On the way up Loveland Pass, the brakes gave out. Dad had to turn the truck around on the narrow mountain road, and we got back to a cabin to spend the night. The next morning my father managed to catch a ride over Loveland Pass to Georgetown, Colorado, where he got a mechanic to bring him back and fix the brakes. So, once again, we continued our trip up to Loveland Pass.

MY *Life* ON THE *Prairie*   FERN MILLER NILSON

As we stopped on top of the pass, Dad soon wanted to start down the mountain. The thin air was affecting his heart. We were very anxious on the descent down Loveland Pass about the heavy load and the steep road with hairpin curves. We hoped and prayed the brakes would hold. What a prayer of relief and thanksgiving we offered when we made it safely down the pass.

On the way home, Dad would take the mattresses off the fruit at night, and we slept on them on the ground under the stars. No one complained. We were together as a family, and we were safe.

One day as my sister and I sat in the narrow space in the back end of the truck, the wind blew a pillow out of the truck. There was no way we could get the attention of Dad and Mother in the cab. They could not hear us when we called to them, so Edna climbed to the cab on top of the load to get their attention. Dad stopped and we went back for the pillow. When we arrived home at Stratton, Uncle Ivan came over and helped unload the truck. The fruit was sold to those who wanted fruit for $1.00 a bushel. We also took some to the store to sell.

In the early 1940's, we took a two-week trip to Yellowstone National Park and on to Washington state to visit Uncle Stanley (Mother's brother) and Aunt Maud at Yacolt, Washington. Uncle Stanley liked to write poetry and was the Poet Laureate of Washington state. After visiting them, we went on to Portland and then down the coast to the Redwoods in California and on home by way of Reno, Nevada. This trip was longer than others had been because of the war. Dad said that this would probably be the last trip for a long time because of that war. He also thought this might be the last trip together as a family since Edna, the oldest of us children, had graduated from Stratton High School.

Mother

Mother greatly missed the trees that were so plentiful in Michigan and Ohio. She worked hard to plant trees in the yard. She always had a nice yard. In the spring, the lilacs and spirea and snowball bushes were in bloom with all the tulips, narcissus, jonquils, snowdrops and other early spring blossoms. When the flower catalogs began arriving in early spring, she enjoyed going through them and ordering new colors and varieties of flowers she did not have.

My Mother

My mother loved her flowers. I am sure she had more flowers than anyone in that part of the state. Living in the country away from the road, few others could enjoy their beauty. It did bring her joy, though, when people and groups would drive out to see the flowers. One time as I walked in her yard, I counted 250 colors of choice iris, but she also specialized in peonies, dahlias, and all other kinds of flowers. Mother entered many flower shows and took home nearly all the blue ribbons.

When they moved to town, they took many of her flowers and planted them in the shape of a large "M" for Miller in their flower bed. Others were planted around the house.

There was a large cottonwood tree on the lawn at the farm. The driveway on the south side of the yard was lined with American Elm trees. Mother also worked hard to plant fruit trees in orchard. She had a very large orchard of all kinds of fruit. In addition, she had a large garden with all kinds of vegetables. The food that was canned from both the orchard and garden supplied us through the fall and winter months.

Mother enjoyed painting with oils. Her upturned basket of red roses and bumblebees was always my favorite. It hung above the piano in our home.

My Mother often quoted sayings to me when I was a child. Making them a part of our lives has become a lost art:

--Early to bed, early to rise, makes a man healthy, wealthy, and wise.
--A bird in the hand is worth two in the bush.
--To obey is better than sacrifice.
--If at first you don't succeed, try, try again.
--Things done by halves are never done right.
--A wise man changes his mind, a fool never.
--Many hands make work light.
--A stitch in time saves nine.
--And the list goes on and on……

Blizzards

Blizzards were another force of nature to reckon with. There were many blizzards each winter when the snow drifted around the buildings and covered fences. Sometimes the drifts had beautiful patterns from the wind and had a crust hard enough for us to walk upon. We did not have storm windows on the farmhouse so the bedrooms in the early years were cold. Jack Frost painted some beautiful scenes on the inside of our windows during the deep cold of winter.

It was easy to get lost in a snowstorm. One evening as Dad and Maurice came from town, they had to bypass the drifts on our private road and drive across the field. In doing so, they thought they were heading straight for the house but later found they had been driving in circles in the field. Only when Mother became alarmed that they had not arrived and turned on the yard light did they see a glow of light and find their way through the snowstorm to the house.

One of our biggest blizzards came on March 31, 1949, my Father's 59th birthday. The snowdrift in our yard between the house and the granary was as high as the peaks on the roofs. I was teaching in Stratton at the time and needed to get into town so I could teach my class. The neighbors helped dig out the snowplow so it could open up a road for all of us to use.

The blizzards of 1949 were the worst the state of Nebraska had ever known. They had begun in Nebraska the fall before, on November 18th, followed by the

Christmas storms. Then, the January blizzard struck between January 2-5, the weather bureau calling it the worst ever experienced in the state from the standpoint of snowfall, wind, and duration. Scores of thousands of

Blizzard of 1949

Train buried by blizzard, 1949

persons were trapped in their homes, many without food, fuel, or medicine. Families sacrificed their furniture to feed feeble flames in kitchen stoves as snow piled high over the windows.

Against the storm the state threw all the resources it could muster, and when that proved inadequate, the Fifth Army tackled what Major General Lewis A. Pick termed the greatest bulldozer operation since the Ledo road.

The full damage probably will never be totaled. Roughly $5,000,000 was spent for snow removal. Cattle losses topped ten million dollars. Dollar losses to retailers were beyond computation.

Railroads were drifted shut with entire engines and railroad cars buried in snowdrifts. They spent millions of dollars in an often-futile struggle against the driving snow. Transportation in the state had never before been so completely paralyzed.

"Operation Snowbound" freed 79,454 snow-bound persons in Nebraska alone, opened 33,973 miles of Nebraska roads, and "liberated 1,782,877 head of livestock. For many farm families, the blow was doubly severe. Some had not succeeded in digging out from the November 18, 1948 and Christmas storms before the January blizzards came in 1949.

Snowfall was officially measured at 30 inches (and two and three times as much unofficially) in many places as much of northern Nebraska was buried by mountainous drifts. In the McCook area, east of Stratton, all roads in and out of town were blocked. By the next day thousands of motorists and train passengers were found stranded in farm houses, small towns, and railroad stations.

Dust Storms

The Natural Resources Conservation Service (NRCS) said this: "Over seventy-five years ago, one of the worst dust storms in history ripped across the plains. This "Black Blizzard" was the result of intensive tillage and wind combined with drought that left the soil open to erosion. Lured by the promise of rich, plentiful soil, thousands of settlers came to the Great Plains. They plowed up native grass and practiced intensive, non-rotational farming. During "the good years," above average rains produced bountiful wheat crops. Soon all farmers were being paid good prices for their commodity. Between 1925 and 1930, the amount of land under cultivation (farming) more than tripled.

Then, two things happened that created disaster. In 1929, the stock market crashed, the price of wheat went from $3.00 a bushel to only 40 cents a bushel. And, in the summer of 1931, the rains stopped, causing the catastrophic drought that renamed the region "The Dust Bowl."

The NRCS also stated that "By December 1934, more than 100 million acres of cropland had lost most or all of its topsoil. Ninety percent of the crops surviving the drought were later destroyed by grasshoppers in an 11,000 square mile area."

I had never seen a dust storm until it hit without mercy on April 14, 1935. Too much land had been broken up to raise more and more crops across Oklahoma, Kansas, Nebraska, and the Dakotas. Farmers had cleaned their fields of all weeds those years. It was the mark of a good farmer to have well-tilled, clean fields. The farmers, including my Father, wanted no weeds or ground cover left in the fields. Dad even would burn off the wheat stubble before planting seed for the following year. Wheat was planted in September and came up, but there was not enough ground cover to hold

1935 Dust Storm

the soil, so the driving winds that swept the soil soon picked it up and blew it across the midwest states. The precious topsoil had first been picked up in Oklahoma and Kansas, carrying it toward Nebraska, where our soil was added to the dust storms.

I was in country school when the first dust storm hit with all its fury on April 14, 1935. I had never seen anything like it. The air was so full of dirt that it got dark by 2:00 that afternoon. I walked to an open window to try to breathe. Soon, Dad came to our country school to pick us children up and take us home with the car lights on. We had no electricity in our schoolhouse so our parents came to get us. We drove home across the wheat field. It was gone. The dirt had been blown away from the little wheat plants and we knew our crop was gone for the next year. The entire farm had been planted to wheat.

As we drove into the yard, the bushes were drifted full with soil. What devastation had taken place so quickly. Red dust from Oklahoma covered the floor of our front porch.

As the dust storms approached, they looked like a black wall, stretched across the sky, boiling and churning as they approached. It was impossible to keep the dust out of the house. We had a fairly new house, but nothing could keep it out. We scooped it off the window sills into dustpans; we brushed it off the walls and curtains. Every inch of woodwork and floors had to be cleaned.

With the next storm, the entire clean-up process had to be repeated. The storms seemed to come so frequently and blew relentlessly with such fury for days. We wondered if they would ever stop. Sometimes we would see them on the horizon and knew they would soon be upon us. Finally, we took brown paper tape with glue to seal all the edges around the windows (it was a terrible job to soak off) and put cloths under the windows as they were locked down. Carpets were cleaned with a Bissell sweeper. It could not possibly pull out all the dust so when we did our spring cleaning, we laid the carpets on the lawn and beat the dust out with a carpet beater.

The wind blew more than soil. Russian thistles (tumbleweeds we called them), raced across the farm land, blown by the tireless wind.

In later years, my favorite Nebraska author was Bess Streeter Aldrich. In her book, **Spring Came On Forever**, she wrote,

> *"...in the Republican Valley the dust...came in clouds, a scourge rolling eastward like reddish-yellow gas across no man's land. Too long in the country farther west, men had torn at the earth's vitals, ...too many times had the edge of the plow gone into the lands which were meant for grazing. There were sections out beyond toward western Nebraska where schools were closed, traffic paralyzed, business suspended, street lights shining all day through the murky atmosphere."*

And in her book, **A Lantern in Her Hand**, Aldrich wrote,

> *"...the room was dense with dust clouds...buildings shivering in the onslaught of dirt...driving home was like swimming the waves of a dirty sea, slowly crawling over the prairie, through the dense dust clouds. The storm was like a blizzard in its fury—a black blizzard, with grit and dust for snow and with field dirt for the drifts through which they drove...eyes and ears were full of the gritty earth particles, And at times it seemed that they would suffocate."*

It was difficult to breathe during those dustbowl days when the air was so full of dirt. I remember standing at an open window at school gasping, and trying to get enough air to breathe. It was a frightening feeling to not be able to get enough air.

The Miller Basin Tiller

The "dirty 30's" were a time of great concern as we lost our crops and good topsoil. Farmers had to use new methods of trying to hold the soil. It was a difficult lesson to learn. They learned that clean fields allowed the wind to erode the valuable topsoil. They began strip farming, summer fallowing, and tried to conserve precious soil moisture.

As a conservation measure, the government was asking farmers to conserve moisture. They wanted to use this practice to deter more dust storms. So in 1939. my father together with his brother, Oscar, invented and manufactured the Miller Basin Tiller. The Miller Basin Tiller made depressions in the soil to hold the rain. These machines were manufactured in the old Brumley Building, to the west of Grosse's Store in Stratton.

The construction of the Miller Basin Tiller apparently was a joint invention by both Dad (Gustaf) and his brother (Oscar) because they made a Joint Patent Application in 1939 to manufacture a "Depression Forming Agricultural Implement."

Being in business together necessitated the forming of a corporation which was called Miller Manufacturing

Company, Incorporated. Dad was president of the corporation; Oscar, vice-president; Mother (Hazel), treasurer; Alta (Oscar's wife), secretary; and Roy Miller (Dad's youngest brother) was the fifth member of the Corporation.

The Basin Tiller made "pits" or "depressions" in the soil which held the rain. This prevented the loss of soil moisture. This business did very well. When the Miller Basin Tillers were first made, tractors had steel wheels. When rubber-tired tractors began to be used, they jolted and bounced as they went over the pits, and the tractor drivers could not stand the jarring, rough ride. Otherwise, the Miller Basin Tillers would likely have been made for a longer period of time.

So, the corporation was dissolved. When Mother and Dad were both in town working at the shop, we children went along and rode tricycles and played in the building or on the sidewalk. Sometimes we would walk to the Drug Store to spend some pennies on candy or ice cream.

The Miller Rod Weeder

Some time later, The Miller Rod Weeder was being used by farmers. It was a square rod mounted in steel shanks which ran underground to kill weeds. It rotated to keep removing the roots and debris to keep the rod clean. This type of machine would not penetrate hard soil so Dad experimented with placing "pointed flat teeth on a bar to make an aggressive bar." This adaptation allowed the Miller Rod Weeder to work well in hard soil. Oscar saw Dad working with it and incorporated it with the revolving rod which was needed to keep the bar clean. It proved to be successful. Thus, it was my father's "idea" that allowed the manufacture of Oscar's Miller Rod Weeder. The Miller Disc would come later.

Floods

As if the spring of 1935 had not dealt us enough blows, another natural catastrophe struck the night of Memorial Day. We had spent the morning, as we always did on Memorial Day, attending Memorial Day Services at the Veterans' Memorial Hall before driving to the Rose Hill Cemetery to decorate family graves.

That evening a big storm came up in the west. Lightning flashed constantly from south to north across the horizon. The heavy rains had started in eastern Colorado flooding the Arikaree and other streams as they moved eastward. They all overflowed and poured into the Republican River resulting in the devastating Republican River flood. By the next morning, the river was a mile wide as it roared down the Republican Valley carrying with it houses, cars, cattle, and people. People clung to trees and debris waiting to be rescued. Many were the stories told of experiences people went through. That morning we drove to the north end of our pasture to watch the flood waters. We were completely cut off from town as there was not a bridge left across the river.

Until the flood, we had driven north, using the road

that bordered the east side of our farm, crossing a bridge over the Republican River (just north of Floyd League's home), then across the railroad to Highway 34, and west into Stratton. As with all the other bridges up and down the river, our bridge, too, was gone. We had no access into town to get mail or groceries. It took a long time for the flood waters to go down and the recurring storms to cease before bridges could be built.

Roads and bridges were not all that was washed away. Much of the railroad had to be rebuilt, too, and many of the towns had flood damage. The southwest section of Stratton was flooded, but Dad's business was not under water.

In the meantime, when the water subsided enough, footbridges were built over the river south of Stratton so families could get into town to get food and supplies. Because our road was washed out, we drove north across our pasture, then crossed the creek, and finally crossed other farms to get south of town. There was no bridge across the creek, either, as it had never been used as a road, so we drove down the bank on one side and up the opposite side. It was pretty steep and sandy. I thought many times we would never make it. Some places in the pasture were pretty sandy, too, especially on one hill, and we had to keep going so we would not get stuck in the sand.

Footbridges were another frightening experience for me as a ten year old. They were about 12 inches wide and often had a wire to hold onto as we walked over the raging water. But frequently they were washed out as high water came down the Republican following more rains, and sometimes there was not time to get a new wire put up to hang onto. Once, when there was nothing to hold onto, I got halfway across when I got frightened and dizzy from the churning water and had to lie down on the narrow board until someone came to get me.

We parked our car on the south side of the river, as everyone else did, walked the footbridge, and then were met by a pickup from Porter's store that was there waiting to take us into town. When we got to town, we purchased our groceries, picked up our mail, and took care of business. When we were ready to go home, Porter's pickup would take us back to the river and helped carry our groceries across. We bought big orders of supplies because we were never sure when we would get across again.

The first bridge built across the Republican River was at Trenton, Nebraska. Then, we could drive to Stratton by way of Trenton. Eventually, two bridges were built south of Stratton for the river now had two channels instead of one. The bridge never was replaced where we used to cross because the river was too wide there to construct a bridge. So, from then on we had to go south of the river to get to Stratton, either through Diehl's land or by taking the south route past Hawkinsons and Pierces.

Our First Tornado

During this period of years with floods and dust storms, we went through many violent storms and saw tornadoes. The first tornado I remember seeing was following a hail storm one afternoon. There had been some rain, but mostly hail. Because the hail was fairly large, we children went out into the yard when the storm subsided to pick up hail to eat. Edna, my oldest sister, looked up toward the sky and said, "Mama, look at that stocking hanging down from the sky over the house." It was the first tornado we girls had ever seen. It never came completely down but went back up into the cloud. I could not understand then why Mother was so concerned about the cloud and called the shop in town to tell Dad. The destructiveness of tornadoes was new to us children until that time. Verna was quite small and went inside to hide behind the door so the tornado could not find her.

My Father Is Protected

As another storm came up one afternoon, Dad came in from the field as it approached. He tarried outside long enough to anchor down a chicken house that had a mother hen and baby chicks inside. Before coming into the house, he stopped by the windmill that stood at the corner of the house. My Father was a storm watcher. He always wanted to know what part of the storm was coming toward our buildings and the farm. As he watched, a voice, from God or an Angel, seemed to say, "You had better get in the house." But he still tarried outside watching the storm a bit longer. Again, it said, "You had better move!" This time he obeyed and just moments later a roof was torn from a small building and landed on the very spot where he had been standing just moments before—but he was safe. God had watched over him and protected him from being injured or killed.

Another Storm

Another time when a storm was approaching, Mother hurried to the basement on an errand. Since the approaching storm looked pretty ominous, she had resolved within herself to pray for our protection when she got back upstairs. She told me that on the way upstairs, a voice, from God or an Angel, seemed to say to her, "You had better pray." And, she thought, "I'm going to when I get upstairs." But the voice said, "You had better pray now!" So, she told me how she stopped halfway up the stairs and asked God to protect us from the storm that was raging outside and, as she did, a tornado destroyed the granary on our farm and left the debris to the south of the house. Again, God kept us safe as a family.

Lightning

There were times of violent lightning during storms. It was especially frightening if the wheat fields were ripe and ready to harvest. Lightning could set the fields on fire. Since my father was a "storm-watcher" I knew that Dad would be watching the storm no matter what time of day or night it came up, and I felt secure knowing that. Also, we knew that Mother and Dad would be praying for our protection.

Several years later our pasture was rented to Lee Carter for a time. One day as the truckers had loaded his cattle out to take them to market, Dad told them to go on. He would walk down the corral and close the gate.

As he started down the corral, he told me that he noticed some unusual lightning on the north divide, about 25-30 miles away. The reason the lightning attracted his attention was that instead of the bolts of lightning going straight down to the ground as they normally do, they were shooting straight out sideways and straight up above the cloud. It was such an unusual display that it attracted his attention, and he marveled at the wonder of it. It was so marvelous that Dad thought within himself, "God, You can just do anything! It's as easy for you to send the bolts of lightning straight out sideways and above the clouds as it is to send them down to the ground." And as he stood there praising God, a bolt of lightning came out of the top of the cloud, he said, and traveled the 25-30 miles sideways and struck the ground beside him, not ten feet away. He was standing in the bright sunshine and yet its brightness was dazzling.

As he told me about it, he said there was no doubt in his mind but that God simply sent His Glory to show His thanks for Dad taking time to praise Him!

Other Disasters

There were other disasters that struck in my early years. Grasshoppers could descend on the area suddenly and completely strip all crops and trees of their foliage.

Several years Jack Rabbits were so thick that they ate the crops off for a distance into the fields. The men would go out at night with car lights and spotlights to shoot the rabbits. The bright light would blind the rabbits and make them easy targets to shoot. Many were the times when they would come home with a trunk full of rabbits.

We fed them to the hogs when we raised hogs on the farm.

At times, coyotes were a menace. Hunts, too, were held to help get rid of them. Sometimes, we would hear the coyotes howling during the night. Frequently, they would go to the watermelon patch to eat into the melons.

The Weather

The weather affected every aspect of our lives. The size of our crop depended on the amount of rain, when it came, and how it came. My father stood at the windows watching because storms could so quickly ruin a year's work on the farm. Our back porch was glassed in as we got older, and I can remember all of us standing at the windows. Storms in southwest Nebraska often came up from the northwest or southwest with a wall of dark cloud and dust boiling ahead of the storm. We would watch it moving from the north divide, across Stratton some five miles away, and finally across our farm. They looked ominous and were so often violent. When the wheat was headed and almost ripe, we feared to have the hail come and in a few minutes destroy our crop. A greenish cast in the cloud always meant hail. Sometimes we would stand outside and hear the roar of hail not far away. After such a storm, the air had the smell of mown straw.

We did not pull our shades at night since we had no one around us, so we saw the terrible lightning at night when storms came up. The lightning bolts often were so close as they struck time and again. When they struck the telephone lines, they would cause the phone to ring. One morning, after a terrible storm, we had no phone. Dad could not see that our telephone line coming in the half-mile from the road was broken, so he climbed up into the attic. There, he found that the lightning was so hot in the night when it struck the line that it had burned the wires in to, in two places. It was a wonder the house did not catch on fire. We felt protected so many times.

Our roads to town were dirt roads until we got to the highway where there was gravel. The dirt roads became very slick and the ruts were terrible after big rains. It was almost impossible to hold the car on the road.

Other Business Interests

At one time, Dad bought and sold wheat on the Chicago Board of Trade. He also appraised farms for the Federal Land Bank for several years to make extra money. I had assumed my parents had taken out a loan with the Federal Land Bank when they bought the farm, but Dad told me in 1976 that he had borrowed money from a local farmer at Eustis, Nebraska, to buy the farm, taking out the Federal Land Bank loan later. The legal land papers confirm this.

In the 1940's and 1950's, my brother, Maurice, and Dad had Hereford cattle in the pasture. At one time, they had up to 180 head of cattle, including calves. Maurice rode over the pasture on horseback as he checked out the cattle from time to time.

Later, they rented the pasture to Lee Carter for several years. After Lee Carter, the pasture was rented to John Diehl. Maurice was always involved in making sure the pasture was rented.

The Miller Disc

The Miller Disc was developed about 1945. This was Dad's biggest invention. He had always had an inventive mind. If he needed something, or something didn't work to his satisfaction, he made what he needed. He told me that most of his inventions took shape as he lay in bed at night. This was the year that I stayed home from teaching to help him in the office.

Dad's discontent with the performance of a disc that he had bought caused him to change the design. The primary disc design, up to this time, was the "single two-way disc" that left ridges at the outer ends and a furrow in the center. By placing one gang behind the other in an off-set manner, Dad was able to make a disc that did a very good discing job and left the ground level without ridges. He tried for a patent on the machine concept, but was unable to get it because of a usage of a vaguely similar concept on a horse-drawn tool many years prior, although that was not the same machine. The "off-set" style of machine he built is today used for aggressive discs.

The Miller Disc

The Business is Sold To Maurice

My father retired from manufacturing at the end of 1955. The business was operated as a partnership between his son, Maurice, and his son-in-law, Dwight Pierce from 1956 through June 1958, Then, it was sold to his son, Maurice on July 1, 1958.

Maurice greatly expanded the business. To accommodate the expansion, he constructed a large, modern building that entirely filled the north half of the block and extended to the highway. He also bought other properties for storing equipment, supplies, and many large trucks to deliver the discs and pick up supplies.

In 1977, he further expanded the business by building a million-dollar plant in Grand Island where he later moved the center of the business. The company sold discs around the world. Later, because of a poor farm economy and high taxes, the business sold its assets to Milfarm Manufacturing Corporation, which continued the product line as "Miller."

Stratton High School

I enrolled in Ninth Grade at Stratton High School the fall of 1937 when I was 13 years old. Dad drove me to school every morning on his way to work at the shop. I usually walked down to the shop at noon to eat my lunch with Dad. On the way back to school after lunch, I often stopped at Grandpa Miller's house. Occasionally, Grandpa Miller would ask me to play the piano when I stopped at noon so he could sing hymns from the Church of God Hymnal. Grandpa loved to sing, and he sang with lots of enthusiasm and volume.

I did well in high school. I took a business course and excelled in typing and shorthand. I have used the typing skills all my life but shorthand was soon outdated by new technology.

I looked forward to my high school graduation. Commencement week began on Sunday evening, May 18, 1941, as we seniors marched into Baccalaureate to "Pomp and Circumstance." Senior Honor Convocation was held on Monday afternoon and Class Night on Monday evening. At the Honors Convocation, I received a scholarship to Hastings College. At Class Night, I read our Class Poem. Commencement was on Tuesday evening, May 21, 1941, and was held at the Veterans' Memorial Hall. I was ranked fourth highest scholastically in the senior class and given a "Scholarship Ranking of A." I graduated from high school when I was 16 years old. I did not yet have a driver's license. Years later I returned to Stratton for the 50th and 70th Reunions of our high school class.

College Days Begin

In the fall of 1941, Mother suggested that I go to McCook Junior College and study to become a teacher. When I registered, I majored in Education but took all of my electives in business, so I almost had a double major. I still liked typing and office work and knew I could always use that training if I needed a job. At one time I thought about working for my father in his manufacturing shop.

I studied Education with Jessie Cleveland who was head of the Education Department. She must have thought I was capable because when they needed a substitute teacher in one of the McCook elementary schools while I was in college, she asked me to take a temporary position. I received all A's on my report cards from McCook Junior College.

Fern, 1954

I had to walk everywhere I went, whether to college or downtown. I had no car during any of my college years. It was nine blocks to college, and also that far downtown. Facing the north wind on cold winter days was difficult, especially when carrying books.

As I returned to college on Sunday, December 7, 1941, I learned about Japan's attack on Pearl Harbor. A somber mood settled over the students as they learned our country was at war. Gas was rationed, so were tires. The speed limit was set at 35 miles per hour to conserve gas.

Sometimes during my second year, I rode part way home on Friday afternoons and Dad would pick me up. I thought we would never get there going 35 miles an hour. It was so slow. Occasionally, on Sunday afternoon I took the "Puddlejumper" back to college in McCook. "The Puddlejumper" was a one-car train. Then, I needed to walk to where I stayed, some nine or more blocks carrying my luggage and food. I thought my arms would break. I felt I should be economical and not take a taxi. I was very lonesome my second year as I rented a basement room and ate alone. The college did not have dormitories at that time.

Teaching

I graduated from McCook Junior College May 24, 1943. I was 18 years old and began looking for a teaching position. I planned to teach that fall in a country school because that was where I would have the best chance to find a job. I was concerned, however, about driving to the country schools in bad weather because there were many hills and the dirt roads had no gravel.

Later, I found that during those war years schools in towns were so in need of teachers that they would accept a teacher with only a two-year teacher's certificate. So I drove to Trenton, Nebraska to talk to the Superintendent of Schools. He informed me they needed a sixth grade teacher. I applied for the position. A few days later he called to say I was hired to teach the sixth grade at $1,005 a year. I was thrilled to get the position in the county seat. My first class had 28 students and when I began teaching I was only 18 years old!

I began the school year with lots of confidence. I had no doubt I could teach the class and handle the students. I just assumed they would respect and mind me as their teacher—and they did!

My classroom was on the third floor of the building and I had many stairs to take the students up and down the three flights. The students never gave me any problems.

My sixth grade had some good baseball games during recess. If the game was at a crucial point and the bell rang calling us in from recess, my class would want to have a longer recess to finish the inning and I would let them. They appreciated my letting them have a longer recess to finish their game. We would work extra hard when we went back to our classroom. The last day of school, I was the only teacher in our building to receive a gift from their class. I was very happy to have the support and respect of my students during my first year of teaching. I taught in the Trenton Schools for three years (1943-1946).

After school started that fall, I met other teachers who lived in the Hurst Apartments at the north end of Main Street, next door to the Post Office. I moved in with Frieda Albert. We had a two room apartment—a kitchen and a living room with a sofa that opened up to a bed at night. Elfie Edwards and Audrey Hoyt lived next door.

The four of us walked to school together and did other things together. Every Thursday evening we took turns entertaining the others in our group for supper. At noon on school days we ate our main meal at a café for 40 cents per dinner.

My teacher's certificate was good for only three years. Every three years teachers had to go to summer school to renew it. Instead of going to summer school, my father asked me to stay at home and do his office work. I did for that one year. That was the year Dad was working on the patent and invention of his disc. In the meantime, I took some night classes at Benkelman, Nebraska and went to summer school at the University of Nebraska to renew my certificate.

In the fall of 1947, I was hired to teach in my home town of Stratton. I felt that was an honor for me. I taught five years in the Stratton schools. Besides teaching I did accompanying for the music teacher. She was the wife of the School Superintendent and directed some wonderful musicals like "The Nutcracker Suite" and "'Twas the Night Before Christmas." I also played for other programs and school graduation exercises.

In the spring of 1953, I realized that life was rather limited for me in southwest Nebraska, so even though the school board at Stratton said that I could have continued teaching in their schools indefinitely, I decided to take a big step and applied to teach in Lincoln, Nebraska. I was hired and taught fourth grade for three years in the Riley and Sheridan Schools.

During the years I taught, our school days were spent almost entirely learning the basics of all the subjects the students needed to learn, such as reading, arithmetic, history and geography. I did, however add some special topics to some of the subjects and, as a class, we made some special creative gifts at holiday times.

I continued with my desire to instill the love of poetry in the lives of my students.

Just as we had studied some of the famous poets and their writings in the country school, I wanted to continue this phase as I taught in town. Poetry was beautiful and I came to appreciate not only the poems the poets penned, but the subjects they wrote about. When you learn some of the great poems from memory, they become a part of your life and stay with you all down through the years. I can still quote many of those poems from memory.

As a teacher, I gave my students the same opportunity to study some of the great poets. I believed English was more than nouns and verbs, subjects and predicates; it was also literature. I realized my students would not retain all the verses, but they would always recognize the titles and parts of the verses they especially liked.

If there was ever a poem that taught the boys and girls the virtues of kindness and selflessness, it is the poem entitled, "Somebody's Mother." No child could study it and not recognize how important it is to help a person who is in need, especially an older person like a grandmother.

SOMEBODY'S MOTHER

The woman was old and ragged and gray
    And bent with the chill of the winter's day.
The street was wet with the recent snow,
    And the woman's feet were aged and slow.

She stood at the crossing and waited long,
    Alone, uncared for, amid the throng—
Of human beings who passed her by,
    Nor heeded the glance of her anxious eye.

Down the street with laughter and shout,
    Glad in the freedom of "school let out,"
Came the boys like a flock of sheep.
    Hailing the snow piled white and deep.

Past the woman so old and gray
    Hastened the children on their way,
Nor offered a helping hand to her,
    So meek, so timid, afraid to stir,
Lest the carriage wheels or the horses' feet,
    Should crowd her down in the slippery street.

At last came one of the merry troop,
    The gayest laddie of all the group;
He paused beside her and whispered low,
    I'll help you across if you wish to go.

Her aged hand on his strong young arm
    She placed and so, without hurt or harm,
He guided her trembling feet along,

Proud that his own were firm and strong.

Then back again to his friends he went,
    His young heart happy and well content.
She's somebody's mother, boys, you know,
    For all she's aged and poor and slow;

And I hope some fellow will lend a hand
    To help my mother, you understand,
If ever she's poor and old and gray,
    When her own dear boy is far away

And "somebody's mother" bowed low her head
    In her home that night, and the prayer she said
Was, "God be kind to the noble boy
    Who is somebody's son and pride and joy."
        --Mary Dow Brine

5th and 6th Grade Class, Stratton School, 1947-1948

During my 11 years of teaching, we did some special things in the schools. At Christmas time we always made a gift for the students to take home to their parents. One year, the janitor cut glass so we could make pictures to take home. We painted designs on the back of the glass., then put a backing sheet on the picture and bound them together with binding.

Another year we made candle centerpieces. I purchased 50 pounds of wax from Standard Oil Company. That year my class met in the gymnasium so we had our own heater and outside door which made it possible to make our wax gift. We melted wax on top of the heater and poured it into a large round salad mold for the base. Since it was wintertime, we could open the door and set it outside in the snow. It hardened quickly and we could pop it out of the mold. We then made five star molds with a wick in the center. They, too, hardened quickly and came out of the molds. We placed them on the round base of wax. When the centerpiece was made, we whipped melted wax with an egg beater and frosted the entire centerpiece. These centerpieces made a lovely gift for each student to take home to their parents.

Early in the month of December, we began learning some choral readings that we would give before Christmas. We learned a choral reading of the "Christmas Story" from the Gospel of Luke. We also learned "'Twas the Night before Christmas." We shared both of them for the Women's Club Christmas program and with a class in the high school.

In February, we celebrated Washington's and Lincoln's birthdays and Valentine's Day by making special valentines. We made black silhouettes of Washington and Lincoln and mounted them on a large, pink valentine, then added a bow of pink ribbon.

Each student made one of these valentines for their parents. The class also made extra copies to give to older people in town who would not be receiving a valentine. On a nice day before Valentine's Day, the entire class walked to the homes we had selected and handed each older person a special valentine. That was a special gift.

My teaching days ended when I was teaching a fourth grade in Lincoln. I told my class that I was leaving because I was planning to be married. Many of the class were children of university parents and came from good backgrounds. They knew about weddings and were so excited about my plans. My wedding portrait was in Hovland-Swanson's store window downtown which no doubt excited my class. The students gave me a lovely bowl for a wedding gift.

My son, Edwin Nilson, writes lovely poetry. He wrote the following poem as a tribute to "My Life on the Prairie."

The Country Schoolteacher

Swept across the prairie skies
    of Bess Streeter Aldrich and
Willa Cather's Red Cloud
    is a place in my memory.

For there was a time
    in 1949 when steam trains
chugged to an anxious stop
    in snowdrifts too high to climb.

In another Nebraska year
    the Republican River swelled
almost as high as a rickety
    footbridge that spanned the tide.

And there were many years
    a young girl walked
those country roads
    to a clapboard schoolhouse.

She didn't have but one
    of everything: a school
dress, a church dress,
    and one tomato sandwich.

But she had as many dreams
>   as stars in the Heavens
> wheeling through the skies
>   as fast as a singing windmill.

And so these prairie dreams
>   took root in her soul
> and in the cool sandbanks
>   of cottonwood creek bottoms.

Dreams were for her
>   what dreams are from God:
> good gifts, unbidden,
>   but sure and lasting.

Those dreams took her
>   to teaching children
> not much older than
>   their spectacled teacher.

I remember these things
>   as I write them down,
> much as anyone remembers
>   the best things of life.

I remember them well
>   because I love the
> country schoolteacher who
>   carried her dreams to me.

Now in these middling years,
    I find there is much more
of depth and purpose
    in these memories with you.

You have had a full chance,
    much more than half,
to live your dreams,
    to live your life.

I send my love to
    the country schoolteacher,
to my dear mother,
    the birthplace of my dreams.
              --Edwin Nilson

Our Family's Christian Faith

Life on the Prairie succeeded because underlying each aspect of its growth was a deep faith in God. My family always went to church. Some of my first experiences had their foundation built on God—from prayers of thanks at the table for each meal, for humble acknowledgement of God's protection during many storms, for family prayers each day as we sought God's guidance and direction, and His strength and health to walk through each day with the confident assurance that He would always go before us.

I marvel at the many ways God has used my life on the prairie. Today, I am almost 90 years old. God has given me a "full life." I did not comprehend how much He had done for me until I began reminiscing about my "Life on the Prairie."

--Fern Miller Nilson